Pure Sport

Should you always 'think about it'?
Are you 'only as good as your last game'?
Is it just a matter of 'keeping your eye on the ball'?

As *Pure Sport* will reveal, the answer to each of these questions is not as obvious as you may first imagine. Relying on intuition alone, too often we can reach flawed conclusions as to what is 'good' sport psychology. This second edition of *Pure Sport* uses everyday language and examples to help you travel through the world of sport psychology recognising what actually works, and what doesn't, when it comes to improving performance.

As the title suggests, *Pure Sport* goes back to basics by highlighting practical concerns for those involved with competitive sport at every age and every level – from junior club members to Olympic athletes. Drawing on their considerable experience as both applied sport psychologists and academics, the authors present practical advice and a powerful array of techniques for channelling and harnessing mental skills with the goal of improving sporting performance.

Drawing on the international popularity of the first edition, in this fully updated second edition the authors have taken the opportunity to revamp chapters with new examples and anecdotes, and have made the book even more accessible for those without a formal background in psychology.

Pure Sport, Second Edition is essential reading for anyone with an active involvement or interest in sport. It will help students, coaches, teams and sportsmen and women to sharpen their mental edge and so realise their true potential in sport and through sport.

John Kremer runs his own successful consultancy business, having been a Reader in Psychology at Queen's University Belfast for 31 years. Along with his academic interest in sport and exercise psychology he has worked directly with a wide range of national and international athletes and teams in over 50 sports.

Aidan Moran is a Professor of Cognitive Psychology at University College Dublin. A Fulbright Scholar, he has written many scientific papers on mental imagery and attention in athletes. He has advised many of Ireland's leading professional athletes and teams, including golfer Pádraig Harrington and the Irish rugby team.

Pure Sport

Practical sport psychology

Second edition

John Kremer and Aidan Moran

LONDON AND NEW YORK

Second edition published 2013
by Routledge
27 Church Road, Hove, East Sussex BN3 2FA

Simultaneously published in the USA and Canada
by Routledge
711 Third Avenue, New York, NY 10017

Routledge is an imprint of the Taylor & Francis Group, an informa business

First edition published by Routledge 2008

British Library Cataloguing in Publication Data
A catalogue record for this book is available from the British Library

Library of Congress Cataloging in Publication Data
A catalog record for this book has been requested

ISBN: 978–0–415–52525–1 (hbk)
ISBN: 978–0–415–52528–2 (pbk)
ISBN: 978–0–203–09670–3 (ebk)

Typeset in Bembo by
Swales & Willis Ltd, Exeter, Devon

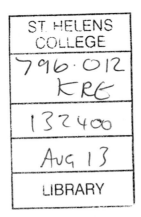

MIX
Paper from
responsible sources
FSC
www.fsc.org   FSC® C013056

Printed and bound in Great Britain by
TJ International Ltd, Padstow, Cornwall

To our families – thank you

Contents

Preface

Welcome to this, the second edition of *Pure Sport,* and the journey through the world of sport psychology that it offers. Before setting off, maybe it's worthwhile laying a few ghosts to rest. First of all, even if you've never heard of sport psychology before, or never met a sport psychologist, make no mistake you will have come across sport psychology. The reason why is because sport psychology is all about the countless ways that the mind influences our performance. Sometimes these effects are obvious and sometimes they are subtle. Sometimes they are planned and sometimes they pop up out of the blue. Sometimes they have a minor impact on how you play and sometimes they can make you despair as to why you ever play at all!

In so many ways it is impossible to ignore the massive influence that our minds have on the way our body performs. Without knowing it, throughout your life a great many people, including yourself, will have been practising a version of sport psychology on you. We are sure that all of us, from our schooldays onwards, can remember those times when a few ill-chosen words, or negative thoughts, took their toll on performance or belief. If you play, watch or manage sport, it is impossible to ignore the influence of the mind on sporting endeavour – but does it have to be haphazard and random? The answer is no. Our goal in *Pure Sport* is simple. It is to help you to use the mental side of sport to your advantage and thereby allow you to explore your true sporting potential.

Along the way, we have tried to act as your guide but with the ultimate target of leaving you in charge, and in a position where you are able to manage your own sport psychology. To help put you in the driving seat, we have tried to cut through the jargon of sport psychology and simply equip you with the basic knowledge, insight and skills to allow your head and body to work together in harmony – to help you, not harm you. We hope that our combined experience as both academics and practicing sport psychologists for nearly 50 years will aid this process.

You will notice that we draw heavily on examples and anecdotes from top-level sport and famous sportspeople. This is to help bring the topics to life but is not to create the impression that the work of sport psychology is reserved for the elite. Precisely the opposite in fact as so many of the messages we offer are tailored not to those who have already reached the top of their game but those who are starting out or have yet to reach their true potential, whatever their current age or performance standard. Remember, even those sporting icons who now seem to glide through the sporting gears so effortlessly were once novices who spent years learning their trade. If we can help you shorten that journey time at all then *Pure Sport* will have been a success.

Since the publication of the first edition of *Pure Sport* in 2008 we have been delighted at the positive feedback we have received from across the world of sport, and especially from those who are still shaping their sporting careers or with little formal knowledge of the subject. This was always our intended target audience and it is pleasing to hear that the book has been helpful to so many. Rather than resting on our laurels, in this second edition we have taken the opportunity not only to revamp chapters with the latest research findings and new examples and anecdotes but also to seek out opportunities to make this material even more accessible for those without a formal background in psychology. We leave it up to you to decide whether or not we have succeeded. We hope you enjoy the journey.

1   Starting out

In modern sport, the gap between winning and losing, the gold or the silver, has never been narrower. The technical resources now available to help players and athletes take their bodies to the physical limits and beyond are breath-taking, and have made that elusive winning edge ever more difficult to find. While physical and tactical preparation has become increasingly comprehensive, there is one dimension of sporting performance that continues to sort the sporting wheat from the chaff, or those who succeed from those who fall short.

You don't need a degree in psychology to know where the answer lies. In the head, or more correctly what goes on inside your head before, during and after competition. How else are we able to explain the ups and downs of performance? On one day you fly, the next day you bomb. Your body has not changed dramatically in 24 hours, your fitness can't have deserted you overnight, and all those skills you spent thousands of hours practising haven't been for nothing – so what has changed? The answer has to be your head, or more correctly, your mental approach.

Take one very obvious example, playing either home or away (see Chapter 8). Wherever you compete, the simple fact is that you will still be playing on a rectangular surface with the same markings, equipment and rules, and against the same number of players – but something will have changed inside your head to make one occasion more challenging. Despite the millions poured into preparation for professional sports, including football, home advantage is still simply taken as accepted, and yet when you think about it, venue is little more than a psychological phenomenon based on the perception and evaluation of different locations.

Making a difference

From the time of the ancient Greeks the significance of the mental side of sport has been acknowledged but of all the sport sciences it is the one that continues to offer the greatest opportunities for making a difference. Whether it's the passionate cry for 'inches' in Al Pacino's famous locker room speech in the film *Any Given Sunday*,[1] or the less emotive strapline of the Great Britain cycling team ('The Aggregation of Marginal Gains'[2]), the message is the same. Making the difference between success and failure is about finding those small margins that can yield that extra one or two per cent.

London 2012 Olympic Stadium (Reprinted with kind permission of LOCOG –
London Organising Committee of the Olympic Games and Paralympic Games Limited)

Pure Sport is about helping you with this process by going back to basics and
allowing your head to work in harmony with your body so that whenever you
perform you give yourself the best chance to test the limits of your physical potential.

We want to eliminate the psychobabble, pull away some of the mystery that
can surround the topic and so make sport psychology understandable and accessible
to those who really matter, the people involved in sport.

By its nature, sport can be unpredictable but there is no need to make it even
more so. For example, are you only as good as your last game? Emphatically, the
answer is no. Simple common sense should tell you that you're actually as good
as your *best* game because that was the occasion when you showed a glimpse of
what you can achieve, when the pieces of the jigsaw all came together and your
physical capability and potential really shone through.

Sadly, through a conspiracy of nature and biology, when left to its own devices,
the head doesn't always work well to our advantage in competitive situations. In

fact, in some respects our heads are hard-wired to conspire against us, as we will explain later (see Chapters 4 and 5). So, our natural tendency is to label those special occasions when it all clicked into place as special, as 'one-offs' or golden times that come along by chance or fate once in a lifetime but which can't be predicted, controlled or repeated.

Furthermore, unless handled with care these occasions can sadly become a burden we carry with us ('if only'), rather than a source of inspiration as to just how good we can be, not occasionally and randomly but routinely.

Total preparation: Giving sport psychology its place

Sport psychology should not be treated as something whacky or off the wall but as an integral part of total preparation, underpinned by a philosophy of leaving nothing to chance. More technically, sport psychology involves all those activities where psychological theory and methods are applied to an understanding and improvement of sporting performance. Sadly however, many athletes' experiences may have been less than positive. Ask Andy Murray, now one of the world's leading tennis players and winner of the 2012 US Open, what he thinks about it and he may tell you about the occasion when he was given a copy of a book by a well-known applied sport psychologist. In the words of his own 2006 Wimbledon blog:

> 'When I was walking to the practice court, a sports psychologist handed me a book he had written. Some people think I am a bit nuts but I don't think I'm ready for a shrink just yet! I had the last laugh – I chucked the book in the bin!!'[3]

Before following his example, could we ask you to reflect for a moment on whether you think that in the past, Andy always had his head and his body working in complete harmony, and therefore whether he always realised his body's true sporting potential? For us, the answer is probably not, although it is noteworthy that things have changed dramatically and positively since his involvement with Ivan Lendl, a man who despite outward appearances has been trying to help him recapture the fun of playing tennis. 'It is fun,' Lendl insists, 'A lot of fun.' 'You feel nervous, obviously. If you didn't feel nervous you'd think there was something wrong. But you have to enjoy being nervous because it's a privilege.'[4]

> 'You work very hard to get there, and so not to be nervous, or to be afraid of being nervous, is a mistake. Once you start enjoying it, that's when you can play well.'[5]

In October 2012, Andy publicly acknowledged the help he had been receiving from a sport psychologist over recent times.

> 'Andy Murray has revealed he has been working with a sports psychologist since the beginning of this year. His coach Ivan Lendl . . . recommended the same woman, Alexis

*Castorri, who helped him. "I spoke about things away from the court that may affect you and stop you from being fully focused on tennis," Murray told BBC Scotland . . . "It's something when I spoke to Ivan [about] at the beginning of the year, he'd travelled with a sports psychologist throughout his career." *[6]

Andy Murray (Courtesy of Inpho Photography)

As another example, the mercurial snooker player Ronnie O'Sullivan once commented,

> '*I tried a sport psychologist once and I never really got anything out of it . . . if you're on, you're on; if you're off, you're off, and there's not a lot you can do about it.*'[7]

Again, a player of fantastic ability 'on his day' but also a player whose performance profile would more closely resemble a roller coaster than a flat plain of consistent excellence.

It is also true that sport psychology has been its own worst enemy. During the 1958 World Cup finals in Sweden, the Brazilian soccer team used the services of a sport psychologist and hypnotherapist who set about 'analysing' pictures sketched by the players. According to Dr Carvalhaes, one 17-year-old player's artistic endeavours revealed him to be someone who was immature, who lacked fighting spirit and therefore did not merit a starting place on the team. Guess who? Pelé.

The good, bad and ugly of sport psychology

Leaving aside these horror stories, on the other side of the coin there are countless examples of those who have either benefited from a positive intervention, or whose mental armoury is already so well stocked that there's no need to add anything else. Darren Clarke, at the age of 43, must have thought that his glory days were past when, in the week prior to the 2011 Open Championship at Royal St George's, by chance he renewed his acquaintance with a very famous golfing psychologist that he had known for several years, 'Dr Bob' Rotella. Bob made no secret of the psychological key that he felt was needed to unlock Darren's undoubted talent. 'I told him, you are going to have to go unconscious.'[8]

Hardly earth shattering advice but simple, sound common sense to help avoid that common sporting disease, paralysis by analysis (see Chapter 5), and advice that helped Darren lift the famous Claret Jug at the end of the week.

By this stage in our careers, we have been fortunate enough to work with literally hundreds of athletes across a variety of sports, from the world's elite in sports including golf, rugby, soccer, canoeing, netball, rowing, badminton, basketball, equestrian sports, Gaelic football, hurling, snooker, athletics, motor sports and squash, to those who have yet to climb the dizzy heights of professional sport. Each intervention, large and small, has been invaluable in helping us slowly but surely grow a stock of knowledge that we now feel confident about applying across all sports and abilities, and that is our aim here. We won't break the confidence of our clients by giving chapter and verse on each engagement but rest assured, the goods on offer have been tried and tested in many different situations.

Having been involved in sport psychology for nearly 50 years, between the two of us we probably feel we don't have too much to prove and that we may have gathered together enough T-shirts to be able to help translate the theory of sport psychology into manageable chunks of practical knowledge for those who are most interested in what works. For those who are more academically minded, there are several good sport psychology books aimed at the 'why' of sport psychology instead of the 'what and the how', and for these readers we have provided a select list at the end of the book.

Why *Pure Sport*?

Speaking of why – why *Pure Sport*? At first glance, this may seem a rather strange title for a book on sport psychology but in fact these two words neatly capture all that the book is about. We have no intention of raising false and glamorous expectations about the mysterious powers of the mind. Instead our approach is purely to help you engage your head with your body and thereby allow you to play your chosen sport to the best of your ability, and what is more, to enjoy the whole experience!

For this to happen, a lot of the baggage that can accumulate during a sporting career may need to be put aside but the person who should be at the centre of affairs has to be the player or athlete. The sport psychologist should never be more than part of a support team that is there to offer advice, but on the understanding that over time the role diminishes rather than grows. Too often sport psychologists have relished the spotlight or have cast themselves as guru or 'doctor'. Both approaches are problematic, the first because the psychologist works best in the background, the second because most sportspeople are not psychologically 'sick' but are just trying to become even better at what they already do very well. The medical model doesn't work, and sets entirely the wrong tone for the relationship with both the player and the coach or management team. A more appropriate approach casts the sport psychologist as a *sport consultant* offering informed advice and support to his or her client to help realise potential, secure in the knowledge that the person will not dread every trip to the surgery.

Doing sport psychology well

Of course, there may be occasions when it becomes clear that a person's problems *are* rather deep-seated. At this stage it can be time to take stock, step aside and instead bring in those who are professionally competent to deal with such matters. By way of example, excessive exercise, even addiction, can suggest a range of psychological problems linked to low self-esteem and body dissatisfaction. Those psychologists with a clinical training are well qualified to identify and treat such issues, particularly when they extend to obsessive-compulsive disorders. Equally, when exercise is being used inappropriately, to control weight or body shape, clinical consequences may not be too far away.

Across the globe, it is unlikely that the demand for sport psychology has ever been higher.[9] However, these powerful market forces can be dangerous and especially when demand outstrips the supply of trained and qualified professionals. In these circumstances caution must be exercised in both promoting and developing sport psychology, with appropriate regulation of those who choose to describe themselves as sport psychologists. In practice, the day-to-day work of a sport psychologist should not be sexy, glamorous or high profile. The focus of attention must always be the sportsperson, and he or she should be encouraged to take responsibility at the heart of affairs, along the way developing a strong network of support that includes specialists from a range of disciplines.

In this environment sport psychology can help athletes to realise their physical potential but make no mistake, it can't make a silk purse out of a sow's ear and shouldn't pretend it can. Fortunately the number of sportspeople who can truly say that they have explored the absolute limits of their physical capabilities remains small and so the future for sport psychology is healthy. When used as part of a long-term development programme, sport psychology can help you look forward to achieving consistent and repeatable good performances. It is less successful as part of a quick fix or crisis management when the wheels are either wobbling or have come off. Instead the most effective work often takes place off season and away from competition where mental skills can be practised, and especially from an early stage in a career.

Who can benefit?

One common misperception about sport psychology is that it is only for the elite, giving them that winning edge when all other angles have been explored. Nothing could be further from the truth. Making sure that the mental and the physical both work together in harmony is a message for all ages and for all levels of ability with the goal of ensuring that whatever potential is there, it has been explored.

If the adoption of some core principles at an early stage of a career can reduce that long waiting time then there will be obvious benefits. There is no need to wait for experience to teach the hard lessons of sport. With careful mentoring these lessons can be imparted early in a career and so a solid and enduring foundation can be guaranteed. At the same time, we should never forget that as Gary Player once remarked,

'You must work very hard to become a natural golfer!'[10]

In many respects the earlier the intervention the better, because by building upwards from a sound foundation, the person can develop the physical and the mental in tandem. Where these are out of synchrony then problems can lie in store, one example being where the athlete's talent starts to bring unexpected rewards. We have both worked with several young athletes who find that what once came easily and lightly has now become hard work as they carry the heavy burden of expectation on their shoulders (see Chapter 2).

To summarise, the goal of *Pure Sport* is not as obvious as it may first have seemed. It is not to foster dependence, nor to blind with science, nor to build confidence to a level that is unrealistic and hence where disappointment is inevitable. Instead, whatever your personal ability may be, the goal is to mould a performance landscape that isn't characterised by peaks and valleys of inconsistencies but by high, broad plains of regular and repeatable good performances.

Gary Player (Courtesy of Inpho Photography)

To use the jargon, the lofty summits of 'peak performance' can be dangerous places to occupy. Those rare times when it all comes together naturally and effortlessly without conscious thought may occur occasionally but they can't be relied on week in and week out. Instead, a less dramatic but more realistic target to aim for could be above average performance, or what is known as repeatable good performance (RGP).[11] This is achievable but only as long as you remain at the head of affairs. You must occupy centre-stage, drawing on whatever resources are necessary at whatever time and place is required, towards the enduring goal of performance improvement and enhancement.

Lurching from game to game, waiting for luck or fate to play its unpredictable role in affairs, is not likely to encourage **confidence**, nor foster a belief in **control**, nor enhance long term **commitment**, and increasingly it is recognised that the healthy balancing of these three Cs will characterise a mentally strong athlete (see Chapter 2). When these three elements work together in a healthy state of 'harmonious interdependence' then the sport psychologist can relax and walk away with a degree of satisfaction, a job well done.

2 The winning mind

It would be tempting to begin this chapter by describing a magic formula for the winning mind. Unfortunately, life isn't that easy. For years, the question of what makes a champion has remained unanswered by sport psychologists and it's probably no coincidence that the earliest documented sport psychology intervention in the 1930s was an attempt to identify the winning mind, or more specifically, the psychological profile of a champion baseball player.[1] This and many subsequent attempts failed miserably. Instead, the honest answer that we keep coming back to is that there simply is no magic psychological formula, instead '*It depends*'.

A quick reflection on the varied personalities of those who have succeeded across the wide world of sport should be enough to show you that the search for a single formula is doomed to failure. Instead, what is shaped through a combination of nature (your genes) and nurture (your experiences) is a set of characteristics and mental strategies that will help you realise your physical potential, and continue to realise that potential throughout your life.

'I didn't get where I am today by talking to a sport psychologist'

To some, the mental strengths that generate athletic success can't be learnt. In other words, you either have it or you don't, and those who obviously do are often keenest to keep the rest of us in our place by letting us know we don't! We disagree and firmly believe that the resilience to deal with the ups and downs of a sporting career can be taught – so long as the right ingredients are brought together in the right way.

Sadly, if left to our own devices, our heads won't always help us because it seems that we are programmed to protect our egos at the expense of learning lessons from our mistakes (see Chapter 7). In other words, we blame failure on all those things out there and beyond our control – the pitch, weather, opponents, referees – and look to boost our egos by taking credit for success. Fortunately, if we are willing to challenge this natural inclination we can learn to draw on both our successes and failures in a way that strengthens character and hardens resolve for meeting future challenges.

Ultimately, mental toughness, along with so many psychological characteristics relating to sporting success, isn't the preserve of the fortunate few but can become the right of many. Sadly, from our experience it is often true that those athletes who are most resistant to these messages are often those who would have the most to gain. Arrogance can be a thin veil disguising a lack of confidence or low self-esteem but it can stand as a real obstacle to progress – and without a genuine willingness to engage and learn then improvement is impossible.

That said, there are others whose resistance may be entirely justifiable not because they are afraid to learn but because they already have the T-shirts and trophies to prove they have what it takes to succeed at the highest level. As the South African golfer Gary Player put it, rather less politely,

> *'When you need to put a two iron on the back of the green to win the Open, how is a psychologist going to help you? If he hasn't got the experience what can he tell you? I'm not totally against psychologists but you have to do a certain amount yourself.'*[2]

In some cases we would agree and especially where there is nothing to be gained from disturbing a winning formula. As the saying goes, 'if it isn't broken, don't fix it'. However, perhaps it is a brave person who feels they have absolutely nothing left to learn, and even the great Gary Player did admit that he was not totally against the occasional word of advice.

Learning to succeed

Although champions do not share a common personality type, they do have some characteristics that not only put them at the top but keep them there. One is very basic but probably the most critical of all: an unswerving capacity to move forward. Put another way, whatever has been achieved is never quite enough, there's always more. A related characteristic is the capacity to cope with pressure and to rebound from failure, allied with a determination to persist in the face of adversity.[3] Even the very best can be beaten and when they are, it is how they come back that matters most. In the famous words of Vince Lombardi, legendary coach of the Green Bay Packers American football team,

> *'It's not whether you get knocked down, it's whether you get back up.'*

Indeed, most top athletes would admit that it is not their triumphs but their adversities (and how they conquered them) that really made them what they are today.

Beware the label

All too often we have found that promising careers in sport have been nipped in the bud because of an ill-timed comment to the effect that the person does or doesn't 'have it'. Labels stick ('She's a natural'; 'He doesn't have the bottle') and once applied the labels can be very difficult to peel off. In the Western world especially we can be far too quick to apply labels. For example, a study looking at why Asian children are so good at maths found one simple factor explained differences between East and West. It wasn't teaching techniques or resources, it was simply the absence of labels such as, 'He's good at sums', or the opposite 'She's not mathematically minded'. In the absence of labels, Asian teachers took it for granted that *all* their pupils had the potential to succeed and so the journey could be undertaken with optimism.[4]

As with sums, so with sport. Without knowing it, we can quickly consign players to the bin by applying labels that stick. As one example, this is what the former British and Irish Lions captain, Brian O'Driscoll, once said about rugby players:

> *'To me, mental strength is a thing players have or don't have. I mean, you can see huge talents coming through, but you know who's going to make it and who's not. It's down to their mentality. It's something that a lot of the public can't see. But players see it. You just know . . . when the going gets tough they want to stand up and be counted.'*[5]

He may be right, but if he isn't then the consequences for talent development are immense. With the greatest respect to one of the most talented rugby players the world has ever seen, the safest option may be to assume that mental skills and techniques *can* be developed, in the same way that physical skills can be sharpened with practice. Yes, of course there are limits to potential but surely it's better to travel hopefully and explore what those limits may be rather than passively accept the vagaries of the fickle finger of fate?

As a counterbalance to Brian O'Driscoll's comment, take the attitude of 2011 400m hurdles World and European champion, Dai Greene. A person who struggled with epilepsy and many other challenges from an early age, he feels he has grown his mental strength by dealing with adversity, and by leaving nothing to chance in his preparation. According to Dai,

> *'My confidence comes from that preparation. I know on the start line I've done everything to be ready . . . A lot of people have superstitions – but I don't need a lucky teddy or to put my shoes on in a certain order. I believe in myself . . . Malcolm [his coach, Malcolm Arnold] thinks you can either handle it or you can't. Personally I think you can learn how to handle it and I've been moulded by personal experience.'*[6]

Staying hungry

A second characteristic of the winning mind is hunger – but a peculiar kind of hunger that never goes away. When managed with care, this hunger fuels success – but it must be controlled. The 2010 BBC Sports Personality of the Year, jump jockey Tony McCoy, admits in his 2011 autobiography that the hunger which drove him relentlessly onwards in the early years of his career verged on the pathological.[7] Always his own fiercest critic, win or lose he would carefully dissect each race to identify what he could have done differently, and Tony was always more preoccupied with his failures than his successes, which he rarely enjoyed for long. He now feels that, although his hunger never goes away, his young family has helped give him a more balanced perspective on life and through which he can manage his hunger more effectively.[8] Or as he said himself,

> *'I used to be very hard on myself . . . Whereas now I just think, "I've made a mistake, try not to let it happen again."'*

Following from the words of Tony McCoy, here is one additional piece of advice: learn how to reflect honestly on defeat but never forget how to celebrate success. The celebration has to be an integral part of the event and without due acknowledgement of a job well done then the journey can quickly become less enjoyable and sustainable.

As a friend and renowned Gaelic football player and coach once remarked, a chip on the shoulder is plenty – but there's no need for the whole potato. For example, because reality never matches up to the heights of expectation then there is the potential for disenchantment, even sulking, and consequently losing motivation. Some of the most highly paid professional sportspeople have shown themselves to be guilty of this crime, not rising to the challenges posed by adversity but instead retreating into a grumpy world of blame and self-recrimination.

In all these cases the key has to be balance – keeping the edge or chip but keeping it in balance. It is often said that an athlete never truly matures and gains a sense of perspective that allows sport to be given its proper place in life until he or she comes through the other side of a significant life event. Bear in mind that Jack Nicklaus, probably the greatest tournament golfer of all time and certainly the greatest battler on the back nine of a golf course, didn't manage to win a major until after the death of his father.

Bradley Wiggins has a sure fire way of keeping himself grounded before he races: he looks at his thumbs. Tattooed on both is the capital letter B, to remind him of his two children, Ben and Bella.

> *'When I'm on the start line of an Olympic final I look at them and think, you know what? This ain't life and death. So all I can do is try and do my best. Nobody's going to shoot me if I don't win. And at that moment I go, "Let's do it."'*[9]

Travel light

To carve a successful sporting career obviously you need talent in the first place but beyond this there are ways you can help stay on track. Many young people set out on their sporting journey for no other reason than they just happen to be good at sport. As time goes by, almost inevitable their ability will be spotted – and what happens next can be just as predictable. Their talent will lead them into a competitive system that can start to take on a life of its own. In the process, an activity that was once fun and enjoyable may soon start to feel heavy and more

Bradley Wiggins (Courtesy of Inpho Photography)

like work. The burdens of expectation rise as the level of competition increases until eventually the lightness and vitality of youth become buried under the weight of a sporting career.

In many respects, what has happened is that the naïve innocence of youth has become infected not only by personal anxieties and ambitions but also by the collective dreams of those who live in hope. These are not always the puppet masters of sporting fiction or the reviled 'pushy parents'. Such people exist, and believe us, they can be scary – but fortunately they are in the minority. More often people are sincere, well meaning and highly motivated parents, teachers, coaches and relatives who want no more than the best for those they care for.

Sadly though, these best intentions can end as a recipe for disaster and dis-appointment. The high drop-out rates from sports such as swimming, dance and gymnastics bear witness to the damage that can be inflicted, and the careful nurturing that is required to sustain interest and enthusiasm through the teenage years.

One thing that can change over time without you realising it is that motives and expectations change. Too often in the past we have come across young players and athletes who have lost the ability to enjoy their chosen sport and who 'play heavy' as a consequence. Sport is littered with examples of those who either gave up or had to rediscover the joy of sport at some later stage of their career, often after they had gained a sense of perspective about the truly important things in life. Interestingly, the legendary basketball coach John Wooden, who died in June

2010 aged 99 years, claimed that a crucial feature of successful sports teams is that they have players who not only work hard but really *love what they do.*[10]

Rory McIlroy went through a difficult time at an early stage of his professional golfing career, managing to throw away an almost unassailable lead in the US Masters in 2011. From the depths of despair, two months later the 21-year-old managed to conjure up an imperious victory in the US Open at Congressional (see also Chapter 7) and went on to win the Shanghai Masters and Hong Kong Open later in the year. What had happened in the meanwhile? One significant event may go some way to explain the transformation – Rory went to Haiti. As a UNICEF celebrity ambassador, he delayed his preparation for the US Open to keep his commitment to visit the shanty towns of Haiti in the aftermath of the earthquake that devastated the island. His own words at the time reveal the personal impact the visit made on him:

> '*If you ever hear me complain about a hotel room again, do give me a clout, won't you?*'[11]

Since his remarkable runs of success in 2011 and 2012, how will he cope with his new found celebrity status, and can he stay 'grounded'? Watch this space but the omens are positive, despite the well-publicised changes in his lifestyle. Following his run of success, and after the split from his long-time manager, Chubby Chandler, McIlroy commented honestly about his career to date, and his willingness to continue to learn:

> '*Yes, I'm surprised by it all and I am making mistakes which, hopefully, I am learning from.*'[12]

At some time in their career, young sportspeople eventually tackle a simple question that may never have even occurred to them in the past – what am I doing here? If the answer is not immediately to hand then problems will lie in store, and performance will suffer.

Two key questions are critical in laying the mental foundation for success. Any hesitation in coming up with an answer to either of these questions needs to be examined to find out the source of interference:

Why am I doing this?

Who am I doing this for?

Why am I doing this?

The answer has to be for pure love and enjoyment. There is nothing complicated about playing sport for love or enjoyment of the activity itself but other motives inevitably come along to muddy the waters. It could be that you are doing it for other people, for status, for money, to sustain a lifestyle, for ego – all these motives come at a cost as pure love of the activity itself becomes a casualty. This is not necessarily true of other motives such as challenge, competition, fitness or companionship where the sport itself remains paramount and the other motives are fortunate consequences of engaging in that activity – but love or enjoyment must still lie at the heart of the matter.

Who am I doing this for?

Again the answer has to be 'pure', purely for yourself. If this ever fades from view or you feel that others seem to be benefiting more from what is happening than you, then there is a need to step back, reappraise, and find a way of occupying centre-stage once more. This does not imply that a family row or worse must ensue but often subtle but effective techniques can be used to sort things out.

This is not being selfish, because success benefits everyone, but it is about rediscovering roots and remembering that when everything else is put aside that sport is fun and is inherently selfish – but in the nicest possible way. The rewards that come along with a successful career in sport may be welcome but they are no more than side effects and to give them more status than they deserve will not improve performance.

Coping with success

Later chapters will explore these issues in more depth but for many players and athletes, ironically it is not failure but *success* and *winning* that create the biggest problems. Vince Lombardi was one of the most successful American football coaches of all time and is remembered for many things, not least his many one-liners. One of his most memorable was,

> '*Winning isn't everything, it's the only thing.*'

Shortly before he died of cancer in 1970, it is rarely reported that he openly acknowledged the danger of adopting this 'must win' mentality. In his own words,

> '*I wish to hell I'd never said the damned thing. I meant the effort, I meant having a goal. I sure as hell didn't mean for people to crush human values and morality.*'[13]

In some respects this is a sad epitaph for a great man but it is also an honest acknowledgement that a healthy sense of balance or perspective on winning is necessary. Put simply, winning *does* matter – but not to the exclusion of all else. Perhaps the following quotes from Vince Lombardi's website more accurately reflect the man, his approach to sport – and to winning:

> '*The object is to win fairly, by the rules – but to win.*'

> '*If it doesn't matter who wins or loses, then why do they keep score?*'[14]

Money, money, money

Especially in the modern world, one of the inevitable side-effects of being successful in sport can be the material benefits and celebrity status this brings. In sport, money is often the root of many evils, and the storyline is not new. The Ancient Greek games eventually died for one reason more than any other: professionalism and money. According to a noted historian it was a combination of the two that promoted the message, 'At all costs avoid losing'[15], and when winner takes all then fear of failure becomes a burden that even the most hardy can find hard to shoulder.

Undoubtedly the greatest darts player of all time Phil 'The Power' Taylor went through an uncharacteristically lean spell some years ago. Despite having engaged the services of a sport psychologist, he was finding it difficult to rekindle his enthusiasm and his famed killer instinct – until his manager Barry Hearn had the wit to recognise that his new found wealth was interfering with what he did best, play darts. His advice was simple. After every tournament he told Phil to lodge the cheque in the bank on a Monday and then forget about it. In other words go back to basics, 'Think poor'.[16] In his own words,

> *'I've seen a lot of sports people over the years – including dart players – where the money has come into it and ruined their careers. Yes, I've made a bit of money but it doesn't make a scrap of difference to me. If I won £50m on the Lottery it would just go into the bank and then it would be "just move on to the next tournament."'*[17]

The rest is history. According to Taylor, the game is what matters most and the tougher it gets, the more he loves it, as the following quote reveals so clearly:

Phil Taylor (Courtesy of Inpho Photography)

'With darts it's just one against one, it's blow for blow. The only thing I could compare it to is boxing. It's dead exciting. You're reacting to each other, the adrenaline's pumping. You don't feel calm at all. But it's all about being able to win when you're pumped up. People say you don't play the player; I play the player every time. It's about reading the body language. I can see it in other sports. I can see when people's minds are wrong. You can see when a footballer's going to miss a penalty. In darts you wait for that dip and then you hit them hard.'[18]

Over the moon?

So, fame and fortune can eventually interfere, but so can too much success too soon.

Both Neil Armstrong, the first moonwalker, and Buzz Aldrin, the second, struggled psychologically coming back down to earth after the Apollo 11 mission because, let's face it, the rest of their lives was destined to be an anti-climax. Sport is littered with examples of bright young stars who burned brightly but briefly and ultimately failed to realise their undoubted promise. Dealing with such early success can be far more troublesome than dealing with failure because the scope for intervention is limited when there is no motivation to do anything while the good times roll.

It takes great discipline and strength to acknowledge the need for support in these circumstances and too often the chance is not taken. Dealing with failure, by contrast, is more straightforward so long as the individual is shown the way

Apollo 11 Crew (Courtesy of NASA)

forward. It is at this juncture that good coaches, mentors and teachers really come into their own in shaping fledgling talent.

Less dramatically, it could be that earlier, sudden improvements in performance become less pronounced as a career progresses and as practice no longer reaps the same immediate rewards, or the practice itself becomes a chore. Once the buzz of discovering potential has dimmed and reality slowly creeps in then the person may have to come to terms with the physical limits of his or her potential.

In team sports, this can be less problematic as the older player can continue on a journey to explore the team potential and maybe take on other roles to help support the team or club. However, in individual sports the reality check can be especially hurtful. The next chapter in particular may be helpful in showing how these difficulties can be dealt with effectively.

Taking a break

Another obstacle that almost every sportsperson will encounter at some stage of their career will be enforced rest or absence through injury. Where there has been a huge personal investment in a sporting life then the adjustment to either rest or retirement can be traumatic. A number of psychological models based on the grieving process have been developed to help understand this process. In a far more positive vein, it is possible to see a period of enforced absence from sport not as a '*time out*' but as a '*time to*', for example as a time to develop other skills including the mental.

A time of injury can be used to return not in shape but in even better shape, and this is a theme to which we will return in Chapter 7. For example, when Roy Keane, the former captain of Ireland and Manchester United, suffered a career-threatening cruciate knee ligament injury in 1998, he was forced to undertake an arduous programme of rehabilitation. During this physical recovery time, he benefited considerably by working on his upper-body strength in the gym, reducing his alcohol intake and by establishing priorities for the remainder of his playing career. Remarkably, as he acknowledged in his autobiography, 'A bleak period in my professional life had changed me . . . time spent alone helped me figure myself out.'[19]

Ending?

At the far side of the sporting career may lurk a whole new collection of mental pitfalls. As for retirement itself, the pain of sudden loss can be intense and to be honest, can't be sidestepped. This is especially true where the person's sense of identity and whole lifestyle has been rooted in their sport. Instead, when the time is ripe there can be opportunities to see how that energy and expertise can be reinvested – but timing here is critical. Too soon and the rawness of loss may carry emotional baggage that interferes with rational decision making. Too late and the sense of identity may have reformed around alternative activities.

In many professional sports the end can be sudden and brutal as age takes its toll. To the outsider the fall from grace can appear dramatic and with no safety net to break the descent. From the inside it is rare that signals have not picked up that time is running out and while denial may cloud judgement usually there is a moment when a choice has to be made – do I jump or should I wait to be pushed? Research has considered the consequences for those who have not made the professional grade in several sports, including American football, basketball, baseball and soccer. Interestingly, the findings show that being released from a contract is not always as traumatic as may be imagined, and most players eventually settle for a level that is appropriate at that stage of their career.

Coaches and managers must also deal with the end and, once more, timing is all. In a profiling session we carried out with coaches from many sports, one of the most critical characteristics that coaches openly identified was 'knowing when to walk'. In many sports, short-term goals dictate that a coach or manager must produce instant results and when these don't appear then room for manoeuvre can become cramped. 'Reading the runes' in these circumstances can ensure departure is planned and dignified – rather than rushed and imposed.

Sport psychologists often find it difficult to work with more mature athletes and especially the successful sportsperson who has been there so often that he or she feels there is nothing more to learn. Or alternatively, the person who is struggling to come to terms with physiological changes associated with ageing and so vainly tries to recapture lost youth, often by pushing harder and harder but for diminishing returns. As one eminent coach once remarked, eventually there is only one solution for veteran athletes, the humane killer – but not always. Take the case of Fauja Singh who, on Sunday 16 October 2011, at the Scotiabank Toronto Waterfront Marathon achieved his dream of becoming the first person aged 100 years to run a marathon, his eighth but maybe not his last.[20]

Travelling hopefully

At each stage of a sporting career different issues and challenges will emerge and these can so easily derail the unwary. This is not an easy road to travel but with a few signposts and clear directions it can be a worthwhile and rewarding experience, with every step of the journey itself to be relished.

To look forward to this trip, one of the most important points to keep in mind is that you travel through a constantly changing landscape. For example what worked or motivated you as a teenager will be quite different from what will inspire you later in life, and so the orientation at each stage of the journey must be dynamic and responsive but throughout there will be one constant that should never change – a sense of who you are.

The person who begins this adventure won't be quite the same as the one who ends it but constantly striving to be someone else along the way will not help. Role models have their place – but they should be kept in their place. We can watch and learn but beyond this a role model can do more harm than good to self-esteem when we imitate or model rather than learn from. Modelling assumes uncritical acceptance, learning involves a more active process of filtering.

In a similar vein certain sports have adopted the stance of 'doing what *they* did' to try to achieve success. That is, identifying a successful team or nation and then attempting to replicate that blueprint, for example by importing 'foreign' coaches or styles of play. Rarely has this strategy yielded long term results. Instead, a more likely outcome is a team with a confused identity, and a heightened sense of inferiority as the role model remains just beyond their grasp. Cultures cannot be imported. The alternative is far more appealing and realistic – by all means, beg, borrow and steal but always remain true to yourself.

The underdog

As money continues to be poured into the pursuit of success in both amateur and professional sport it is too easy to buy into the idea that resources will always win out, and that success can be bought. With this in mind, many teams and individuals participate or travel to international tournaments as underdogs, with no expectation of success because the form book tells them so. Rubbish! As long as that belief persists then the formbook will prevail – but as long as there are those who are driven to tear up the form guide then sport will continue to prosper.

In 2009, Leinster approached the final of the European Heineken Cup against Leicester very much as underdogs. In the days leading up to the final, one of us was contacted by the sport psychologist (and former student) working with the Leinster team, looking for words of advice. The reply that was given was simple, keep it simple, summed up in three short phrases – 'No Excuses, No Script, No Respect'.

In 2011, Leinster again found themselves in the final but this time not as underdogs but as former European champions. This time the advice we offered was even simpler – 'No psychology', or to be more precise, what we meant was don't over-analyse, don't over-complicate, just go out there and play as you know you can – and they did, remarkably turning a half-time 22-6 deficit around, and eventually winning 33-22!

The underdog label can be used in either a positive or a negative way but from a psychological perspective it has fantastic potential when handled with care. As a negative, it can help maintain the status quo by keeping the outsider firmly in place and the label has hamstrung too many good players and teams over the years. If you let it, the label can provide a ready-made excuse for failure but only if you let it. From a positive motivational perspective, the underdog mentality, a healthy disrespect for authority, can work wonders so long as it is underpinned by a sufficient level of confidence. This does not have to extend to will win – but can win.

Can win . . .

It is a common misperception that the more confidence the better in sport. Unfortunately it's not that simple as the consequences of over-confidence can be disastrous. At heart, 'will win' is fragile as nothing is that certain and entirely under our control. 'Can win' suggests we have the capability with the right motivation and circumstance, and is far easier to sustain in the longer term. 'Can win' is sufficient to provide the drive to 'give it a rattle', and the great advantage of this strategy is that the burden of expectation is lifted from the shoulders of those who are then allowed to go out and simply perform.

Many teams and individuals perform the first part of the underdog trick but often fail at the final hurdle when eventually giving in to the prevailing status quo – otherwise known as GLS ('gallant loser syndrome'). For example, a team that against all odds finds itself leading may then decide that the safest option is to defend that lead. In truth, this becomes the riskiest option as play becomes compressed into little more than a practice game of defence and attack. More rarely, a team will have the self-belief to know that what took them to that point can take them further, and that an honourable defeat is still a defeat and is unacceptable. In other words, when the going gets tough, the tough keep going or keep doing what took them there in the first place.

Some situations allow the underdog tag to emerge naturally but how can you hope to continue to persuade champions that they are still underdogs? This must be one of the greatest skills of sport management but it is one that certain individuals have honed to perfection, constantly creating the impression that the world is 'agin us', including match officials, administrators and the media. Any examples spring to mind?

. . . But dare to lose

Either through such tactics or in other ways, what a good coach or manager is often trying to instil in players is a mentality that while the journey may be tough, the goal is within grasp ('can win'), but it won't happen by chance and, critically, to be able to win you must acknowledge the prospect of losing. In other words, in order to win, Dare to Lose. This is not negative but realistic and actually reflects the coming together of two psychological constructs that have long interested applied psychologists in many fields, including education and industry.

The literature suggests that our need to achieve (NAch) and fear of failure (FF) combine to help determine our approach to competition.[21] Both are entirely independent and so, contrary to popular belief, this means you can have a variety of profiles. Typically, scores are used to classify according to type, as shown over the page.

Not surprisingly, Type 3s often represent the best long-term investment for any sport and have the right make-up to sustain a successful career. Unfortunately the combination of circumstances that draws a young person into a sport, and

Winning and losing 1

TYPE 1 – has a **low** interest in winning but a **high** fear of failing.
These individuals will often leave jobs unfinished or lose interest in activities. They will avoid competition if possible but may choose to compete against someone they know they will beat, such as a younger brother or sister.

TYPE 2 – has a **low** interest in winning and a **low** fear of failing.
These people feel indifferent towards competition and would probably wonder why people make such a fuss about winning and losing. 'After all, it is only a game', they may say.

TYPE 3 – has a **high** interest in winning but a **low** fear of failing.
These type of people love competition, especially where the outcome is uncertain. They are full of energy towards a particular goal and take calculated risks. They love to win but realise that losing is not the end of the world. They are very persistent and highly self-motivated.

TYPE 4 – has a **high** interest in winning and a **high** fear of failing.
These individuals also enjoy competitive situations and take personal responsibility for outcomes, but failures cause self-doubt and lowers their self-confidence. This worry over failing often reveals itself in poor sportsmanship, an unwillingness to take risks, decreased persistence, and sometimes a superficial air of arrogance. As a result of these factors, these individuals often fail to fulfil their potential.

including the part played by significant others, can inadvertently produce not Type 3s but Types 1 or 4. These may then drift towards becoming Type 2s and finally drop-outs from sport.

In terms of actual performance, those with a high fear of failing will often underperform not through lack of ability but through inhibition and an unwillingness to take risks. Poor performances then feed further fear of failure and so create a downward spiral.

The bad news is that many young people do not truly enjoy their sport because of this combination; the good news is that it is not difficult to change this profile but only if the person is willing to change. Unfortunately Type 3s can also be characterised by arrogance and this complicates matters as genuine engagement is not easy to sustain.

These individuals will often have remarkable defences ('Teflon coated'; 'slopey shouldered') that make sure 'nothing sticks', including critical advice or even support. However, if there is a willingness to change then the process relies on going back to basics by rebuilding the primary motives for taking part – for love, enjoyment and for yourself. This could include deliberately sidelining significant others and placing more and more personal responsibility on the shoulders of the athlete. With these foundations, a more solid and secure basis for long-term growth can then be fostered.

How to stay hungry: Hate failure, want to achieve

Looking well beyond the research literature to the reality of sport, the interplay between NAch and FF in determining performance is much more complicated than first appears. Somewhat naïvely, many sport psychologists still advocate a profile based on low fear of failure and a high need to achieve. In reality very often this is impossible to attain, and particularly when the amount of investment in terms of time and effort has been so great that failure has serious consequences. Indeed many top sportspeople would say that the fear of losing is what continues to give them the edge. In the words of Billie Jean King, winner of 39 women's tennis grand slam finals,

> '*A champion is afraid of losing. Everyone else is afraid of winning.*'[22]

Fear can motivate but it can also inhibit and when it does then alternative strategies may be needed. If fear starts to cramp rather than boost performance it may be a

Billie Jean King (Courtesy of Inpho Photography)

case of working to turn fear from a negative emotion to a positive one – *Hatred of Failure* (HF). It is acceptable to hate the prospect of failure and all that goes with it but to be afraid of that prospect is an entirely different matter.

In a similar vein, needing to achieve implies a natural force or drive that is imposed and outside your control. A healthier term may be really choosing or wanting it, *Want to Achieve* or WAch – 'wanting to' rather than 'needing to' may seem a small shift but it represents a significant move in terms of placing you in charge of affairs.

Tackling defences

Already we have identified a number of external factors that can have an adverse effect on performance and motivation but what of internal or psychological mechanisms that can stand in the way of success? Very often these natural mechanisms shield us from harm – and especially when we suffer failure or defeat. Sadly, this short-term gain can prevent us from learning from our mistakes. Before going any further, try this short questionnaire.

Winning and losing 2

Winning

Think about the last time you won a sport competition, match, tournament or game and then indicate the extent to which you feel that each of the following was influential. (Rate each on a scale of 1 to 10 where 1 = not true and 10 = entirely true.)

1. To what extent do you feel your ability was a factor in the result?
2. To what extent do you feel the result was due to your good luck?
3. To what extent do you feel the result came down to your opponent playing poorly?
4. To what extent do you feel the result was because you tried hard?

Losing

Now think about the last time you lost and then indicate the extent to which you feel that each of the following was influential. (Rate each on a scale of 1 to 10 where 1 = not true and 10 = entirely true.)

1. To what extent do you feel your ability was a factor in the result?
2. To what extent do you feel the result was due to your bad luck?
3. To what extent do you feel the result came down to your opponent playing well?
4. To what extent do you feel the result was because you didn't try hard?

If you compare your scores on each of the four questions for winning and losing, you will probably find that you're more inclined to take credit for success and find excuses for failure. So you should find relatively higher attribution scores for internal factors (Q1 and Q4) under winning than losing, and vice versa for external factors when explaining why you lost. What is more, whether the internal factor is stable (Q1 – ability) or unstable (Q4 – effort) and equally whether the external factors are temporary (Q2 – bad luck) or permanent (Q3 – opponents) will all have an influence on future motivation.

If you are like most people, you may not be taking sufficient credit for your successes and so feel that you have relatively little control over results. Whatever pattern emerges, in order to develop 'the winning mind' clearly there are ways of explaining events that will be more effective than others. For example, in order for someone to build on success it is often important to change the way you think about your performance – to work hard at acknowledging that a good performance was not because of luck or chance but reflected on internal factors that are stable (skill) or unstable (effort). Equally, a poor performance should not be excused away but can be drawn on to provide useful learning points that in turn can be translated into more effective practice.

Another word that makes its appearance at this point is *control*. The control that the person believes they have over internal and external factors is vital. Almost all competitors will believe that they can control effort but fewer believe that they can control or influence ability. However, do remember that this must be an optimistic journey where change is seen as possible. In fact we can nurture a winning mind by drawing on our experiences, both positive and negative. High achievers will naturally credit their successes to themselves and their ability, and will deal with failures in various ways, including finding positive ways that setbacks can be dealt with through increased effort and practice.

On the one hand, there may be occasions where there is a need to put your hand up and acknowledge mistakes in order to move forward. On the other hand, taken to its extreme low achievers will always blame themselves for mistakes and defeat, and will believe there is nothing they can do to change the situation. What is more, while high achievers will explain success with reference to stable factors, low achievers will talk about temporary factors beyond their control when explaining success – and so assume that the performance is not repeatable.

Each style then becomes self-fulfilling, generating either a success circle for high achievers or a vicious circle of failure for low achievers. That is, by attributing success to internal factors, high achievers will experience more personal pride in their success and so seek out achievement situations. They will persist and try harder when the going gets tough whereas low achievers do not attribute success internally and so become less motivated over time.

For any coach key lessons can be extracted from this work. From a psychological perspective, the coach's task should be to instil the belief that success relates to effort and ability (internal causes), and that players are capable of again attaining the highest level of skill that they have shown in the past at any time in the future.

Equally, strategies for dealing with failure must resist the temptation to excuse and instead find positive paths forward.

Before leaving this research behind there is one further finding to note in passing. It is known by psychologists as the fundamental attribution error.[23] What this term refers to is the consistent finding that in comparison with those who play, those who watch will overemphasise the role played by internal factors (skill and effort) in explaining results. The disastrous consequences for post-match discussions and arguments should be obvious!

Knowing yourself

So, we explain away successes and failures in ways that are not always productive but forewarned is forearmed and reinforces a key component of the winning mind – the capacity to be honest and self-reflective. The next chapter will explore the techniques involved in more detail; for now the principle is all you need to know. A later chapter will also consider ways in which you can manage stress so as to maximise performance (Chapter 4) but for now remember that the key to successful stress management, yet again, is self-awareness – knowing what has worked in the past and having the techniques and the discipline to recreate that state time and again.

In essence the winning mind works hard to eliminate thoughts of luck or fate and instead takes control, reflecting on previous performances, and especially the 'head' that was carried into those games. This reflection is used to draft a tried and trusted formula for mental preparation. Techniques including use of biofeedback (e.g., pulse rate) and mental training (e.g., thought stopping, imagery) can then be used to hit the zone repeatedly, and to stay there. During play itself, other techniques can be employed to achieve two primary aims – to keep the head in the present (not dwelling on past mistakes; not waiting for the final whistle), and to create an environment where thinking does not interfere with doing.

Strangely, this means that the winning mind needs to know when to think and when not to think. Too often all those countless hours of practice to make the difficult seem natural can be lost when thought interferes, otherwise known as *paralysis by analysis*. Losing confidence often refers to no more than the times when the spontaneous has become thoughtful, and stopping those thoughts is a vital skill – but not a difficult one to develop.

The foundation lies in sequencing and so preventing the contamination of one stage by another. Somewhat crudely, these stages can be referred to as:

> **Feck it**
>
> **Do it**
>
> **Think about it**

1. **'Feck it'** refers to that balanced state of mind where the player performs knowing that all the hard work and preparation is behind and the primary task now is to play unfettered by doubts, worries or expectation – in other words, give it your best shot.

2. **'Do it'** involves making sure that the clock is never turned back during play itself, so that the expert does not revert to a novice by thinking about what should be happening spontaneously, or reflecting on what has happened and especially mistakes. This will only happen if analysis is not allowed to interfere with action, or at least if it does appear, it appears at the right time, for example during breaks in play. A useful trick to remind yourself that analysis must begin and end is to draw a line on the back of your hand before you play – the line signifying whatever has happened is past, quite literally, drawing the line! Or if you are inclined to start taking it all too seriously, why not try a curved line, to remind you not to take yourself too seriously – and that you are allowed to smile at yourself!

3. **'Think about it'** is actually the most important phase, for without this one, the other two are impossible. Depending on the sport in question there may be a lot, little or no time for reflection during play itself. Whatever time there is should be used wisely but the most important thinking time should take place almost immediately, and well before others have an opportunity to judge you. That is the time for a systematic and structured assessment of what went well, what went less well – and what must be worked on before the next time. This can then be used as a reference point for discussions with others on performance and will then frame subsequent practice (see Chapter 3).

Psychologists will often describe their work in terms of **A, B** and **C**. A or *affect* concerns emotion, B is *behaviour* and C is *cognition*, and what this simple strategy actually achieves is a framework for coordinating and prioritising these three in order to produce optimal performance. That is, (**A**) emotionally the individual must be right when entering competition, ready to meet the challenge but not overwhelmed; (**B**) during competition, behaviour should be pre-eminent, with

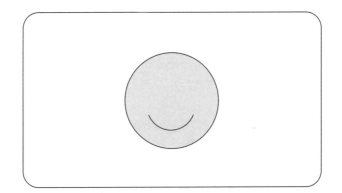

Draw the (curved) line

cognition or emotion held firmly in check; (**C**) afterwards is the time for rational thought (cognition), to reflect and analyse and hence provide the basis for future action. In this way the winning mind harnesses A, B and C in that order to produce effective performance.

Mental toughness: Balancing the Cs

As more pieces of the jigsaw start to fit into place, a clearer picture of the winning mind should be emerging. The image may not be alien to you because it is not about trying to make you something that you are not. Instead the core is you – but armed with a clear sense of purpose, an honest acknowledgement of what you are and what you can be, and equipped with skills and techniques that can make sure that the sporting journey continues to excite you around every bend in the road. With the right guide, mental toughness will then naturally develop as the journey continues.

Balance remains critical throughout this journey. This balance includes four constructs that can help tie together so many of the themes already introduced and that underpin mental toughness. Talk of the Cs is not new in sport psychology but there have been many variations on the theme. The winning mind has the capacity to balance these Cs. A successful athlete will continuously monitor these to ensure that when they act in concert they facilitate performance, and no single 'C' or attribute should ever be allowed to become too dominant.

Confidence, commitment, control and challenge

In the past perhaps too much emphasis was placed on confidence as the most important, when in fact commitment and control should be included as equal partners. Too much confidence can be as dangerous as too little because too much may foster complacency or cockiness which in turn will lower commitment and control. Too little can have the opposite effect. Likewise with commitment. Too much and there is a danger of losing control which will adversely impact on confidence. Too little and the performance will lack passion and hence may be too controlled. In this way, too much or too little of any one and the mix will be unhealthy; keep them all in a harmony and you have a well-balanced athlete who will continue to feel good about what needs to be done and how to do it.

Challenge represents the fourth and encompassing C, defining the overall mental approach underpinning your journey. Each step on this journey should be seen as an interesting test of how far you have come and where else you choose to go. At each stage there should remain that buzz of anticipation because the future is uncertain and the end of the journey is unknown. So the limits of your personal talents can be explored with a genuine sense of excitement and anticipation.

In this environment, change is the only constant as you continue to explore new challenges. And what about those who stand in your way, your opponents? They are interesting obstacles to your progress that must be dealt with, not according to reputation but according to the practical ways in which they prevent you moving onwards and upwards.

The last word

So when all is said and done, what is the winning mind? Forget about a set of psychological ingredients that are magically plugged into your head to make you walk, talk and think like a champ. Instead of describing the winning mind as an object, think of it as a journey of discovery, with you as the main character. As with any expedition, when you begin you will need help to prepare and equip yourself for what lies ahead. As time goes by, instead of taking on more baggage, and guides, your aim should be to learn from your successes and failures, and so lose these burdens and travel lighter and lighter, enjoying the scenery along the way. The winning mind is open to these experiences, learning and growing, with the skills at your disposal to deal with whatever may come your way.

Set against this foundation, the remaining chapters should help to equip you with the right skills and techniques, and as you continue to practise these skills so your role expands as an ever increasing circle.

It's important that you continue to occupy the centre ground, fine-tuning the three Cs (**Control, Commitment** and **Confidence**) but enveloped in a mindset that sees every new experience, good or bad, as a fresh **Challenge**. Meeting these challenges allows you to become secure in who you are, what you are about and

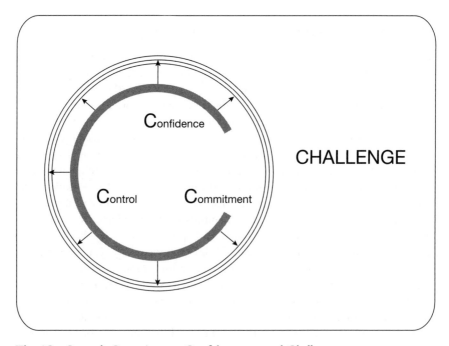

The 4Cs: Control, Commitment, Confidence . . . and Challenge

what needs to be done to constantly find ways of improving. Over time the circle should grow but at the right pace – not as a sign of arrogance or over-confidence but as an indication of growing independence and maturity. Grow the circle too slowly and you have become cocooned in an unhealthy comfort blanket of over-dependence, too fast and you are discarding support before you should. Instead, think of shedding layers of bark – when you need them they protect, when it is time to grow, they no longer serve a purpose.

With all this in mind, let's now move on to the next stage of your journey and back to the future – in Chapter 3.

3   Mirror gazing

We hope that the first two chapters will have helped establish guiding principles for your journey through the rest of *Pure Sport*. In the longer term, these same principles should help to mould a mental approach to sport that will help you explore the limits of your physical potential, whatever they may be. Now is the time to equip you with the tools that will assist you in this quest, and we begin by looking not *forwards* but *backwards* – asking you to reflect on who you are and what brought you to your sport in the first place.

To help this process, one word must be uppermost in your thoughts – honesty. Too many sportspeople can lose their way because they fool themselves, or others, for example by borrowing others' identities, and especially those who have already achieved success.

While it may be useful to learn from others, you must be at ease with who you are and understand what you are. Don't worry, we are not about to plunge you into the world of psychotherapy – that can be a journey from which it's not always easy to escape. This self-assessment does not have to extend to all aspects of personality or temperament but only those that are directly related to sporting performance. As Chapter 2 makes clear, who you are is at the core of the whole enterprise but we are now concerned with fine-tuning those aspects of what *makes* you what you are to ensure that they help maximise your sporting potential.

In a more pragmatic vein what we are suggesting is that you become familiar with the concept of mirror gazing or honest self-reflection. As the story goes, many years ago a very famous New Zealand rugby player, at the start of his test career, is alleged to have let the rest of the team know exactly what he thought of their poor performances after one particular game. Without realising it, he had broken an unspoken rule among the team at that time. Grabbing him by the throat, the captain shoved his face into a mirror and let him know in no uncertain terms that this behaviour was unacceptable. In fact, no player was allowed to discuss the game until physically he had looked into a mirror and asked himself the question – what did I do for the team? Only then had he earned the right to talk to his team-mates.

A powerful lesson. While we all assess our performances from time to time, it is rare that this evaluation will be thorough and systematic. Instead, quite naturally, we are inclined to be selective, choosing aspects of play that we or others consider

All Blacks winning 2011 Rugby World Cup (Courtesy of Inpho Photography)

to be the most important. If your confidence is high then you are likely to focus on the positives but if your confidence has dipped then you are more likely to highlight your mistakes and weaknesses. In this way you may lose a rounded or balanced picture of performance and come to highlight a small fraction of the total scene. This bias will then influence how you prepare and so the cycle of delusion continues.

The alternative is to begin to use tools to assess what has been done and what needs to be done, and in the process provide the impetus for self-motivation. Performance profiling and goal setting are two valuable techniques for helping an athlete become self-driven or self-motivated but before going any further it may be useful to clarify just what is meant by motivation.

What is motivation?

Ask anyone what motivation is and they are quite likely to talk about the things that motivate us, including the motives that make us get out of bed in the morning and do something. In psychology, similar ideas have long held sway and so, for example, Abraham Maslow famously described a hierarchical set of needs that motivate or drive us to action.[1]

Moving from bottom to top of the pyramid or hierarchy, the needs begin with basic survival then safety needs, belonging, esteem and finally, self-actualisation itself. According to Maslow we are only able to deal with higher order needs once we have sorted the rest.

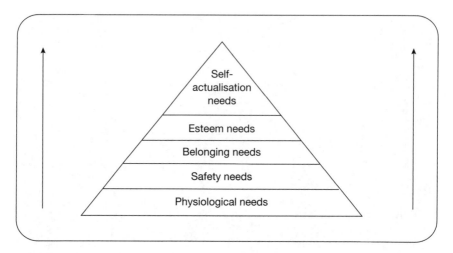

Maslow's hierarchy of needs

The model sounds entirely plausible until you test it against the real world and then you often find that life is not quite so orderly. Basically, we make choices and prioritise different motives at different times. So, for example, the artist may buy canvas at the expense of food, or the explorer may risk life and limb for no other motive than 'because it was there'. These may be exceptional examples but more generally we are far more sophisticated in our decision making and how we prioritise motives than earlier 'content' models of motivation, including Abraham Maslow's, would suggest.

Within sport psychology there have been literally hundreds of studies aimed at identifying the significance of different motives in determining sport participation. With increasing evidence of obesity and related health problems among young people, an urgent priority is how to encourage young people to take part in physical activity of any sort. Intricate models of participation motivation have emerged to suggest that a whole host of variables interact to determine why we take part and continue to participate, with a critical distinction being made between extrinsic motives (doing it for rewards that are outside the individual – money, status, trophies, etc.) as opposed to motives that come from within or intrinsic motives (feeling good, self-realisation, enjoyment).

In general, this research suggests that intrinsic motives are the most powerful and sustaining long term, and that doing something for the sake of the task itself instead of boosting your ego works best. In many ways, these findings have been used to underscore the philosophy outlined in Chapter 2.

In recent years, the literature has moved from simple descriptions of motives and drives towards an understanding of the process of how these factors act to move us.[2] These theories and models make reference to issues that can influence our commitment but the core is simple and is worthwhile keeping in mind. In particular the model is useful for helping you understand and diagnose problems that may arise, including why it is that you or others don't seem to have the same enthusiasm as before, and how this can be remedied.

These models describe motivation not in terms of content but as a dynamic *process* – the how and the why of what we do. The process of motivation is seen to hinge on the relationship between four factors:

Effort	how hard we are prepared to work
Performance	what we do, in training and competition
Outcome	what we get out of what we do
Satisfaction	how we feel about the process

It is assumed that these four elements relate in a systematic way.

To be motivated at all, you must recognise that an increase in the effort you are prepared to put in can be repaid in a positive change in performance – otherwise why bother? However, common sense dictates that an increase in effort does not automatically reflect in improved performance. Ability will play a part, as will the role that you are expected to play – your position in a team or the style of play you must adopt. You may be highly motivated but if you don't have the knowledge and skills, or you are being asked to do something which is inappropriate, then that effort will count for nothing.

Next, you must not only believe that an increase in effort can change your performance but also that change, whether during training or in competition, will reflect in outcomes or rewards that you genuinely value, and including both intrinsic and extrinsic. It is not absolute reward either but what you receive relative to those around you – am I getting as much as, more, or less than the next person? In other words, is it fair and so was it worth the effort? So, for example, if I turn up for training without fail twice a week and work as hard as I can but never receive an acknowledgement whereas he swans in when he feels like it and yet always

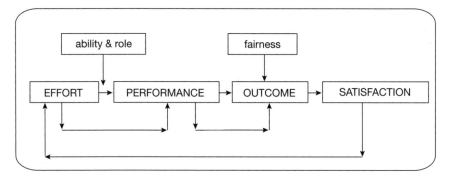

The process of motivation

seems to attract the attention of the coach and is guaranteed his starting place, why should I bother?

Only when you have expended effort, seen the performance and judged the outcomes (including success and failure) do you then evaluate the whole process (was it worth it?) and this evaluation then determines your level of satisfaction that in turn determines the effort you are prepared to invest in the future.

As you look across this process, it becomes possible to spot occasions where the chain is broken or weak and so motivation is lost. Is the problem with ability, perceived ability, the player's role, positive feedback on effort and on good performances, fairness? Each are likely to play some part in sustaining motivation over time.

Performance profiling

Having explained the process of motivation, we must now turn to the practice of motivating and how we can encourage long-term commitment. The technique of performance profiling is now widely accepted across top-level sport as a natural starting point for systematically identifying your strengths and weaknesses. For example, many national sports institutes now routinely provide their elite performers with training diaries or logs in order to make sure that they are able to reference previous performances in moving onwards and upwards – in other words, profiling.

While profiling has attracted most attention in relation to elite sport, it can be useful in a wide range of contexts. What is more it does not have to be restricted to post-performance analysis. At the start and end of a campaign or season, it is a useful way of establishing what has been achieved and what is needed in the future. Also, the same techniques can be used by coaches as by athletes, where exactly the same principles apply.

Various techniques have been used to profile, ranging from the highly structured to the less formal. Almost all identify a list of attributes together with scores, out of say 10, to represent where you are and where you would like to be. Richard Butler, an eminent UK sport psychologist, pioneered the use of an interesting device, the performance dartboard, as an easy visual tool for presenting profiles.[3] Each attribute is assigned a segment of the dartboard and within each segment two colours usually represent the scores of 'where you are' and ' where you would like to be', typically out of 10. While useful, the number of segments on the board restrict the attributes that can be shown to 20.

As an alternative to the dartboard, a simple chart can be used instead. You can list on the chart all the attributes, skills, knowledge, techniques etc. that are relevant to performance, and then honestly appraise where you stand in relation to each one.

To help you understand the process, we will use an example of a young golfer who is keen to win a place on the professional tour. He has already decided that he is willing to give this ambition whatever it takes over the next twelve months,

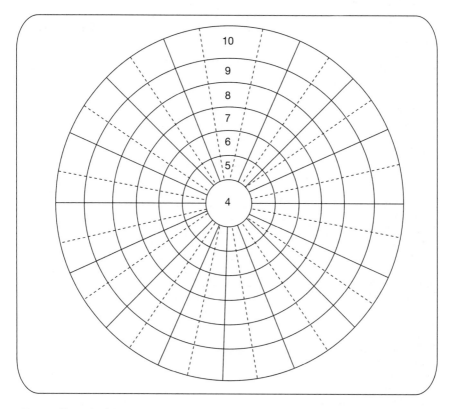

The profiling dartboard

and has the full support of his family and coach. The starting point of his journey involves an honest reflection on skills and attributes ranging across the physical to the mental to the tactical, and including lifestyle issues.

You will note that the list doesn't include core aspects of personality or self-identity but instead focuses attention on those skills and issues that are likely to be directly associated with golf.

The player could first of all complete the left hand column and then the right, highlighting occasions where there is the greatest need for improvement. It is important to avoid the temptation of always putting '10' in the right hand column. A '10' is often unattainable but instead it is more sensible to give a realistic assessment of where it is possible to be by a certain time. Having put down where you stand then it is useful to bring in as many people as possible to give an opinion as to whether the ratings are fair and realistic. The completed scale then provides a starting point for a goal-setting master plan to move from left to right – from where you are to where you want to be.

A profiling master plan

	Where am I?	*Where do I want to be?*
Upper body strength		
Leg strength		
Bunker play		
Putting		
Chipping		
Driving		
Long iron		
Short iron		
Consistency		
Control		
Confidence		
Commitment		
Will to win		
Imagery skills		
Attentional styles		
Lifestyle		
Diet		
Sleep patterns		
Reading a course		
Reading a green		
Club selection		
Shot selection		
Relaxation skills		
Time management		
Fear of failure		
Need to achieve		
Thought stopping techniques		
Physical fitness		
Flexibility		
Knowledge		
Listening skills		
Social skills		
Media/PR skills		

Post-performance profiling

The procedure described above will take time and is designed for longer-term planning. More immediately, after each competition it may be possible to come up with a shorter list that you could use to judge your performance, and before your next training session. Clearly there is scope in such a procedure to introduce attributes that the coach would like to highlight and especially if that is an area that the team really needs to work on. A typical example from a team sport is shown over the page.

By adopting this systematic and personal approach to evaluation you are avoiding all the pitfalls attached to focusing exclusively on immediate or high-profile issues. It forces a more rounded assessment and can also form a very useful basis for

Post-match analysis

	Your performance (out of 10)									
Work rate	1	2	3	4	5	6	7	8	9	10
Distribution	1	2	3	4	5	6	7	8	9	10
Winning possession	1	2	3	4	5	6	7	8	9	10
Reading the game	1	2	3	4	5	6	7	8	9	10
Defence	1	2	3	4	5	6	7	8	9	10
Support	1	2	3	4	5	6	7	8	9	10
Consistency	1	2	3	4	5	6	7	8	9	10
Discipline	1	2	3	4	5	6	7	8	9	10
Team player	1	2	3	4	5	6	7	8	9	10
Communication	1	2	3	4	5	6	7	8	9	10

discussion between the player and the coach or manager. If you are a coach, often it is useful to have the player complete the form alone before sitting down with you and talking through scores and what can be done to bring about an improvement.

For coaches and athletes alike, the techniques are not difficult to learn but, more than anything, require the ability to offer an honest appraisal of strengths and weaknesses. A training log or diary could be used to support these profiles, providing an opportunity to comment on reasons why performance may have dipped or peaked at certain times.

Que sera sera

For some athletes, these profiling techniques will be immediately welcome as they help to reinforce their existing practices based on principles of personal control and agency – doing something about it. For those who are less analytic, there may be more resistance as the uncertainty attached to each performance continues to offer an unhealthy allure.

'*Que sera sera*' (whatever will be, will be) is a sentiment that many sportspeople seem to buy into all too readily. It can be comforting to believe that the finger of fate can point in your direction at some happy and unexpected time and as long as you hang in there, things may change for the better. National lotteries thrive on this sentiment – coupled with our poor understanding of statistics.

Unfortunately this mindset becomes a recipe for inconsistency and not improvement because placing your faith in luck or fate automatically reduces the scope for accepting personal control, and in the process, doing something about it. In relation to goal setting and self-motivation this can create serious obstacles to progress.

Many sportspeople continue to cling to rituals and superstitions before performance in the belief that these will 'magically' reduce the risk of failure. Although pre-performance routines can improve concentration when used properly (see Chapter 5), they can, if used as superstitious crutches, actually increase the risk of failure because they take personal responsibility out of the equation and replace it with an external force or authority.

Dealing with these issues can be difficult and they often have to be handled extremely sensitively. Fortunately, reliance on these rituals will tend to reduce as the foundations of an effective intervention are laid down but they can quickly reappear and especially during times of particular stress, seemingly as a way of 'controlling' anxiety. Again, perversely, reliance on superstition or fate will have precisely the *opposite* effect in the longer term by taking the person out of the driving seat and turning them into a backseat passenger. Anxiety and worry based on the uncertainty of outcome will flourish in this environment.

Before we continue, please do not imagine that we are in the process of fashioning a sporting android, devoid of human feelings and personality. Nothing could be further from the truth. The purpose is quite the opposite, to put you as a person first – but in control and stripped of the baggage that conspires to hold you back. Asking someone to reflect on their performance is not an alien task. We all look back on what we have done well and badly but often we do this haphazardly and in a way that reinforces false impressions. Do it systematically and instead of being a barrier to progress, it becomes an aid.

Setting goals

Having established where you stand in terms of relevant skills, knowledge and attributes, and having identified where you need to be, the next step in the process must involve finding a way of travelling from here to there.

For many years, goal setting has been embraced by business and management consultants who use it as an essential part of motivational training programmes. More recently, sport has borrowed these ideas. Basic goal-setting procedures have become increasingly popular and accessible to coaches and athletes alike, and the principles have been frequently translated into popular language to encourage practical use. Goal setting can work and often does but it is not without its problems and these should not be glossed over. Instead what we intend to do is suggest how these principles may be applied – before issuing a few heath warnings based on our practical experience over the years.

Within sport, goal setting really came to life in the 1970s. Probably the most famous example of a systematic goal-setting procedure was that undertaken by the 1976 Olympic gold medallist, John Naber (see p. 41).[4]

Four years later John Naber succeeded not only in winning his gold medal in the 100m backstroke but also three other golds and a silver medal – and broke four world records in the process.

Interestingly, the most successful Olympic swimmer of all time, Michael Phelps, very publicly set himself the goal of winning seven gold medals in the 2008 Olympic Games, to add to the six he had already won in Athens in 2004. He

John Naber: Realising his dream

John Naber
(Courtesy of Inpho Photography)

'In 1972 Mark Spitz won seven gold medals, breaking seven world records. I was at home watching him on my living room floor. And I said to myself at that time, "wouldn't it be nice to be able to win a gold medal, to be able to be a world champion in Olympic competition." So right then I had this dream of being an Olympic champion. But right about then it became a goal. That "dream to goal" transition is the biggest thing I learned prior to Olympic competition – how important it is to set a goal. My personal best time in the 100 back was 59.5. Roland Matthes, winning the same event for the second consecutive Olympics (1972), went 56.3. I extrapolated this, you know, three Olympic performances and I figured in 1976, 55.5 would have been the order of the day. That's what I figured I would have to do. So I'm four seconds off the shortest backstroke event on the Olympic program. It's the equivalent of dropping four seconds in the 440 yard dash. It's a substantial chunk. But because it's a goal, now I can decisively figure out how I can attack that. I have four years to do it in. I'm watching TV in 1972. I've got four years to train. So it's only one second a year. That's still a substantial jump. Swimmers train ten or eleven months a year, so it's about a tenth of a second a month, giving time off for missed workouts. And you figure we train six days a week so it's only about 1/300 of a second a day. We train from 6–8 in the morning and 4–6 in the evening so it's really only about 1/1200 of a second every hour. Do you know how short a 1/1200 of a second is? Look at my hand and blink when I snap my fingers, would you please? Okay, from the time when your eyelids started to close to the time they touched, 5/1200 of a second elapsed. For me to stand on the pool deck and say, "during the next 60 minutes I'm going to improve that much," that's a believable dream. I can believe in myself. I can't believe I'm going to drop four seconds by the next Olympics. But I can believe I can get that much faster. Couldn't you? Sure!! So all of a sudden I'm moving.'

duly won eight! London 2012 was his last Olympics. And was goal setting still important to the man known as The Baltimore Bullet? As he said in 2011,

> 'The goal I have set for London is a very hard goal. I think it's something that I think I can reach, and it will mean something very special if I reach that. The only two that are really going to know that goal are Bob [Bowman, his coach] and I. We're the only two that are going to put the countless hours in the pool and the weight room.'[5]

Michael duly won four golds and two silvers at the London Olympics, to become the most decorated Olympian of all time (22 medals, 18 gold), before subsequently retiring.

More generally, the use of goal setting as a motivational technique in sport can be traced directly back to a theory initially developed in the world of business.[6] Goal setting research has been carried out in a wide variety of situations but regardless of the type of task or the individuals tested, the majority of studies reveal that setting goals can lead to improved performance. As to why, goals probably have a positive influence in at least four ways. First, they focus attention; second, they mobilise effort in proportion to task demands; third, they enhance persistence; and finally, they encourage longer-term strategies. Furthermore, a number of features relate to these performance effects.

Goal-setting principles

Difficulty	More difficult goals lead to a higher level of performance than easy goals.
Specificity	Specific goals are more effective than general subjective goals (e.g., 'do your best') or no goals.
Acceptance	To be effective goals must be accepted by the performer whether they are self-instigated or assigned by someone else.
Feedback	Goals will not be effective in the absence of feedback.

While not all of us may have the single-minded dedication of a John Naber or other great Olympians,[7] we can still draw on broadly similar principles to establish goals that will lead like small stepping stones from where we are to where we want to be. And having profiled your performance or your skills/knowledge you have already made considerable progress in delivering on goal setting. However, just because you can measure and assess does not mean that you are committed to action so before going any further it is worth pausing to answer the following questions:

What would you like to achieve in your sport?

How important is it to you?

There is no point in punishing yourself unnecessarily; if the goal is really not all that important to you then there is no point in putting in place a regime that is doomed to fail before it begins. This is not an admission of defeat but a realistic and sober assessment of what is important in your life and where your priorities lie. To downgrade sport to a recreational activity and then to invest an appropriate amount of time and energy in something that still matters, but maybe not too much, is fine, and there may still be scope for limited goal setting even in these circumstances.

At the same time, if you do have the commitment to continue to improve, the next stage is to return to the results of your profiling and to identify, one at a time, each item on the list where there is room for improvement, and then to prioritise these items in a sensible way which allows you to draw up a goal-setting master plan.

When is the best time to do this work? It is not during the heat of competition or following a run of poor form but during the close season, when you have had an opportunity to reflect on where you are going and how you are going to get there. This master plan should include a timescale for each skill, attribute or area of knowledge, indicating where you are and where you want to be by a given date. The timescale, start date and end point for each should be tailored, always taking into account practical considerations and including the time and resources you have available. To keep this scheme in your thoughts, this plan could be presented on a large sheet which is pinned somewhere prominently to constantly remind you of your schedule.

From a practical perspective, a *Gantt Chart*[8] offers a simple way of representing different timelines for different goal-setting activities. Many commercial software packages are now available to make the task of constructing a chart very easy. The chart will allow you to see immediately the start and end points for each programme, and also significant checkpoints along the way. They also allow you to describe connections between the various activities. For example, you may wish to develop strength and flexibility before working on a particular skill or routine.

Doing goal setting

Having established a master plan, now is the time to look at each element of the plan in more detail, to work out a goal-setting routine for each element. To do this, for the sake of convenience the principles are often presented as an acronym, either **SMART** (specific, measurable, attainable, realistic and timely) or **SCAMP** (see p. 44). Of the two, we have found that SCAMP seems to capture the principles more completely, and sits easily alongside the philosophy we have outlined earlier.

SCAMP!

S = Specific

Don't set vague goals, e.g., get better. Specify exactly how much you want to improve and how you can measure it. Predict the extent of your improvement and you will work hard to achieve it.

C = Challenging and Controllable

Set performance goals at a level slightly ahead of your current ability; this means that goals are possible but also provide an interesting challenge. Also remember to keep your goals within personal control rather than depending on performance of others (e.g., performance not outcome).

A = Attainable

Don't burden yourself with an impossible goal. All goals should relate to where you are now and you should aim to improve yourself step by step. Don't be afraid to reassess goals if they prove to be unrealistic.

M = Measurable and Multiple

A sense of achievement is greatest and motivation enhanced most effectively when progress can actually be seen. Goals are best expressed in a form which can be measured objectively, e.g., seconds off time. Failing that, measure performance or characteristic on a subjective rating scale of 1 to 10, e.g., rate ability to cope under pressure on scale of 1 to 10. Also, multiple goals increase the probability of achievement.

P = Personal

The goals you set must relate to you as an individual. Decide what you want to achieve; don't borrow other people's goals. This will enhance your commitment to these objectives.

To see what this can mean in practice, we will use the example of a tennis player who decides, among many other things and in consultation with her coach, that she wants to improve her first serve accuracy.

Goal setting in action

An up-and-coming tennis player wishes to improve the accuracy of her first serve. At present she determines that when serving at maximum speed, she is able to hit the ball into an imaginary two-metre target circle in the receiving court three times out of ten on average. She then sets herself a realistic goal of being able to hit this target seven times out of ten by the start of the season in ten weeks time. How does she achieve this? She works out a training programme that involves going to an empty court at her local club three times a week and on each occasion hitting 80 serves, forty shots from each side of the court into four imaginary targets (ten per target) on each visit. She establishes weekly targets and records her performance on each occasion, including subjective rating, and charts her improvement over time. In the light of this continual feedback she is able to check whether she is on line for achieving her goal and can adjust her practice over the weeks if necessary.

Exactly the same principles can be applied to any sport and any skill. The rules of goal setting are simple. By answering each of the following ten questions you should be able to develop a goal-setting programme for every skill or quality that you would like to improve.

The 10-step approach to goal setting

1. Which aspect of performance do I wish to improve?
2. What associated skills/qualities/attributes must be developed?
3. What routines or practices will help me improve each of these?
4. How can I measure each?
5. What is my present level of attainment?
6. What level of performance would I like to achieve by a certain date?
7. What milestones do I want to put in place between the start and the end?
8. What level of performance do I want to reach by each milestone?
9. Who can help me monitor my progress?
10. Who can provide me with expert advice to 'quality assure' the process?

For each item on a profiling list, it may be that one or several goal-setting procedures emerge. For example, under the label of 'flexibility' there may be several stretching routines that you follow for different muscle groups. Nevertheless, the same principles would apply for each procedure. You establish a baseline (e.g., how far beyond my big toe can I reach on a toe-board), you then establish your goal by a given date (e.g., a further 10 centimetres by next month) and then put in place milestones along the way at which time you measure and thereby establish and record progress made (e.g., ticks or stars on the Gantt Chart).

Timetables can and should be modified to take into account changing circumstances including illness, injury or other commitments. Never forget that this procedure is designed to make you feel good about reaching targets; it is not about hurting yourself when you fail. If the programme is too difficult or over-optimistic then always adjust, and never be afraid to seek advice from others.

Some skills or qualities are easy to measure, others are more difficult. Strength or physical ability can usually be measured without too much thought, for example by the number of repetitions, weight lifted or accuracy of performance. However, for certain lifestyle issues the means of measurement may be quite different. Sleep patterns may be no more than recording time to bed and time up, having first established what is an appropriate regime. Dietary assessment may involve measurement of calories or type of food (and it should be immediately obvious that many diet clubs actually do no more than simple goal setting when trying to encourage weight loss).

The assessment of other skills or qualities may require more imagination, and especially in relation to mental skills. However, with skills such as stress management (e.g., timing pulse rate), reaction time (e.g., timing performance on simple and complex reaction time tasks) or mental rehearsal (e.g., checking the match between the imagined and actual time it takes you to perform a certain task), it can be fun coming up with interesting ways to measure and chart performance. When all else fails it may be a question of resorting to a subjective assessment of how you are feeling, or asking others to rate your performance against specified criteria.

You don't have to do this alone. Talk to other people and especially those with expert knowledge to make sure what you are doing is sensible, and try to involve them in assessment at the milestones to reassure yourself that your improvement is not fiction but fact. Ultimately however it is about you feeling good about your improvement rather than waiting for others to applaud.

Goal setting and the real world

So far, all may appear rosy. Goal setting looks like a relatively simple psychological technique that will allow you to maximise your potential through structured planning and training. Unfortunately this optimistic presentation can flatter to deceive, for goal setting is a prime example where popularity is based on *perceived* value but where application has proceeded without an acknowledgement of significant theoretical and practical problems. This is not to abandon the approach but instead to suggest that it will only work and be effective in certain circumstances.

Some problems are linked to the way in which sport differs from the world of work where goal setting was originally developed. For example, there may be obvious differences in the reasons why individuals are actually involved in work or sport in the first place. Principally, the extrinsic rewards associated with work stand in contrast to the intrinsic motivators that are so crucial in maintaining a voluntary involvement in many sports.

A further major distinction rests upon how goal setting is applied in sport and in work, and the relative emphasis which is placed on either *product* or *process*. Performance enhancement in business is normally directly related to an end product – increased productivity. By contrast, sport often emphasises that goal setting should focus on process or performance and not outcome. There is also ongoing discussion as to whether setting distant, long-term goals can actually be de-motivating and so whether there is a need to introduce sub-goals in order to sustain commitment. Our earlier discussion strongly suggests that while the long-term goals may light the fire, it has to be constantly rekindled by short-term goals that are in easy reach.

The last word

Clearly the level of single-minded dedication shown by some elite sportspeople, including former Olympians such as John Naber, would be beyond the reach of all but a dedicated minority, and to put in place such a highly structured programme would be unrealistic. This is where there is a need for a strong dose of realism to ensure that whichever profiling and goal-setting schedules are put in place, they must be tailored to the needs and characteristics of the individual. The flexibility of profiling and goal setting to accommodate individual differences is often ignored and too many schemes have failed as a consequence. Instead, constantly adjust and readjust these motivational tools to meet changing times and changed people.

It is also worth noting that some critics of goal setting claim that it can interfere with competition unless handled with care. For example, in swimming it was noted that some swimmers could be seen to be over the moon even when finishing last in a heat or final because they had met their individual time target. It was as though the other swimmers had dissolved and the race had been reduced to nothing more than an individual time trial.

To counter this dangerous trend, some swimming coaches advocated a shift away from over-reliance on specific performance goals and towards an accommodation of competitive goals, that is, to beat the person in the next lane. It should never be forgotten that many of the techniques we describe in this chapter are a means to an end, and the end is tied to the intrinsic significance of competition itself. This is what makes sport enjoyable, and when the balance becomes tilted so dramatically that winning loses any emotional significance then there are problems.

Does all this mean that goal setting should be abandoned? No, but it does remind us that it is not always the magic solution either. Many highly motivated athletes may not need the rigours of a goal-setting programme to maintain their commitment. In fact, it may do no more than heighten their anxieties and raise unrealistic expectation.

At the other end of the spectrum, there may be recreational athletes who would find the discipline of a regimented goal-setting programme to be more of a turn-off than a turn-on. Ultimately, what we would suggest is that goal setting *can* be a powerful tool for sustaining self-motivation but it should be applied with a modicum of common sense and should be tailored to the needs and circumstances of the individual. There are many variations on the theme and the trick is to find and use that variation which works best for you.

When all else is said and done, every day we spend time reflecting on what has been and what could be – and what is it that separates those who dream from those who achieve? Often it is no more than knowing how to join the two together.

4   Hitting the zone

Whether we're novices or world champions, we are all inclined to feel butterflies in our stomachs when we cross the line to play competitive sport. First and foremost, those nerves or butterflies reveal that competition really matters to you, and it *has* to matter – otherwise why take part in the first place? This feeling is nothing to worry about, though – it's entirely natural. In fact, if you *didn't* experience that sensation, it could be even *more* worrying because it may suggest that you don't really care. Indeed, many athletes use the term 'flat' to describe this experience of feeling sluggish or lethargic in situations where they would prefer to be more 'psyched up'. For example, when golfer Graeme McDowell (Europe), a US Open champion, played Hunter Mahan (USA) in the crucial final singles match of the 2010 Ryder Cup, he felt strangely

> *'flat for 12, 13 holes. Then it became very obvious that the match was going to count.'*[1]

Rising to the occasion, however, McDowell won the match that helped Europe to a one point victory over the USA.

Like most people, you probably don't relish the prospect of being tested and in competitive sport the evaluation that you will experience is not only swiftly delivered but is often publicly observed. Each time we compete we encounter the certainty of evaluation and the possibility of failure. Few of us enjoy failing but competitive sport, by its very nature, embraces uncertainty as to the eventual outcome (good or bad) and regardless of our ability level.

When these factors are taken together, it becomes obvious that competition and nerves must go hand in hand. But the good news is that you don't have to let competitive occasions take over and get the better of you. With the right preparation and outlook, competing against others can continue to be a positive, exciting and rewarding experience, through the good times and the not so good. Let's face it, how else can you really find out how good you are at anything unless you are willing to test yourself to the limit?

At the outset, one point is very clear. José Mourinho, one of the most successful managers in world football, was correct when he claimed that,

> *'Without emotional control, you cannot play . . . you cannot react. You have to be cool.'*[2]

But how can you stay calm and controlled when there's a lot at stake? In this chapter, we'll show you how to stay cool and to enjoy the challenge of sport.

We'll begin by explaining what being nervous means and we'll show why anxiety can be a help or a hindrance in sport depending on how you perceive it. After that, we'll examine some of the factors that make people feel nervous and explore how anxiety affects your performance – paying special attention to the well-known experience of 'choking' under pressure. In the final section of the chapter, we'll show you how to stay cool in pressure situations.

Before we begin, however, let's explore the difference between *losing your cool* and staying cool in sport.

Losing your cool . . . or staying cool?

Sometimes, athletes are so psyched up that they 'lose their cool' and destroy their chances of success. For example, consider what happened to Paul Gascoigne, one of the most gifted English footballers of his generation, in the 1991 FA Cup Final against Nottingham Forest at Wembley. Over-eager to impress his new employers before his proposed transfer to Lazio in Rome, and pumped up excessively by his manic pre-match behaviour (apparently he had upset his team-mates by bouncing relentlessly on his bed and kicking pillows in his hotel room before the game),[3] Gascoigne lunged wildly at an opponent shortly after the match started and ruptured cruciate ligaments in his own right knee. This self-induced injury not only prevented him from playing for most of the following season (1991–1992) but also triggered a downward spiral in his form and health from which he never fully recovered. By contrast with Gascoigne, Tiger Woods, in his prime, thrived on the pressure of competition. For him, playing in pressure situations was a thrilling game – a challenge to his skills:

> '. . . the challenge is hitting good golf shots when you have to . . . to do it when the nerves are fluttering, the heart pounding, the palms sweating . . . that's the thrill.'[4]

In this quotation, Tiger Woods tells us that he experiences exactly the same type of anxiety symptoms (e.g., butterflies in the stomach, a pounding heart and sweaty palms) as the rest of us in competitive situations. But by using words like 'challenge' and 'thrill', he *labels* his nervousness differently from the way we usually do. And how we label experiences influences how we respond to them. For example, Dan Carter, the All-Black outside-half who is regarded as one of the greatest rugby players of all time, has learned to welcome his nervous symptoms before a match:

> 'I had learnt that they (physical symptoms) just emphasised a 'buzz' indicating that I was excited and ready for the game.'[5]

But not all athletes manage to keep their cool when it matters most. For example, the former England rugby star Jonny Wilkinson was renowned for his intense feelings of anxiety before matches:

Dan Carter (Courtesy of Inpho Photography)

> *'From the earliest times I can remember, I've been a very nervous individual – not nervous because of being scared, not physically scared, just frightened of letting myself down or letting other people down or just losing. It just causes that kind of anxiety.'*[6]

As before, this quotation yields several important insights into anxiety in sport. For example, it reveals that feelings of nervousness are usually triggered by psychological factors (such as worrying about not playing to your own high standards) rather than physical ones (e.g., fear of incurring an injury). Also, Wilkinson's quotation shows us that world-class athletes are not afraid to admit that they feel nerves in certain situations. Indeed, there may be an advantage to this admission because, as another sporting champion, the 6-time golf major winner Nick Faldo, wisely observed,

> *'The player who recognises that he is nervous is streets ahead of the fellow who is in denial.'*[7]

Another finding is that nervousness is generally a good thing in sport because it forces you to take appropriate action. Put simply, nerves can energise you by making your adrenaline flow. Tennis grand slam tournament winner Andy Murray, the 2012 US Open champion, highlighted this point when he said that,

> *'Being nervous is good. Having that adrenaline gets your mind focused on the match.'*[8]

Having explored elite athletes' views on staying cool under pressure, let's now examine what 'nervousness' means and what causes it in sport.

'Nerves'

In psychology, nerves or nervousness means having feelings of anxiety – an unpleasant emotion with certain distinctive features. Among these characteristics are physical tension, a high degree of bodily arousal and persistent feelings of worry about a forthcoming event or situation. These symptoms are not accidental. They are part of your body's 'fight or flight' reaction – a warning system that prepares you either to confront an imminent source of danger or else to run away from it. By the way, the term 'anxiety' is derived from the Latin word *angere*, meaning 'to choke'. This original meaning is interesting because 'choking' under pressure (or performing poorly as a result of anxiety) is well-known in competitive sport. We'll return to this experience shortly. At this stage, however, let's explain the six most important things you need to know about nervousness in sport.

1. There are different types of anxiety . . .

First, anxiety comes in different forms. Psychologists distinguish between nervousness that occurs as a temporary experience in certain specific situations (called 'state' anxiety) and nervousness that reflects a long-standing personality characteristic ('trait anxiety' – a tendency to perceive almost any situation as potentially threatening) which can be triggered virtually anywhere in everyday life. Typically, while state anxiety is short-lived and situation-specific, trait anxiety is longer-lasting because it is deep-seated.

We can also distinguish between 'cognitive' anxiety (worries, doubts and pessimistic predictions about the future) and bodily anxiety (physical symptoms such as high arousal and a rapid heart-beat). Interestingly, these different types of anxiety appear to change in different ways during sporting competition. To illustrate, once a match starts bodily anxiety tends to decrease but cognitive anxiety usually fluctuates, depending on how the game is going. For this reason, mistakes in sport are more likely to be caused by cognitive anxiety than by bodily anxiety (see Chapter 7 for a discussion of mistake-management techniques).

2. Anxiety is different from fear

Although anxiety resembles fear there are important differences between these two emotional states. For a start, anxiety usually lasts longer and is more vague or undifferentiated than fear. In fact, anxious people can't always explain exactly what they're afraid of but they can feel a cloud hanging over them or a weight on their shoulders most of the time. Also, whereas you're usually anxious about the unknown, you tend to be 'afraid' of things that you *do* know – such as a steep ski slope in front of you or the prospect of being hurt in a tackle.

Usually, anxiety is triggered whenever you interpret a particular person, event or situation as posing a threat to you in some way. This perception of threat may be based either on realistic or imaginary fears. For example, if you are a golfer standing on the first tee when playing for the Captain's Prize, you will probably feel a little anxious even though realistically, your feelings in this case are completely disproportionate to the actual physical danger involved in this situation. On the other hand, if you are a novice skier facing your first steep slope with no instructor around, you have every reason to feel nervous because of the potential danger of being injured.

3. Anxiety is based on arousal

As we mentioned earlier, when you encounter a frightening situation (one that carries the threat of physical harm), your body activates the 'fight or flight' response – a primitive warning system that prepares you either to confront this source of danger or else to run away from it. This response occurs automatically whenever you *think* that you are in danger, regardless of the reality of the actual threat involved. It includes such bodily reactions as a rapid heart-beat, increased blood pressure, the release of glucose into the bloodstream and a heightened state of 'arousal' or alertness – all of which help prepare you to respond to the anticipated emergency. So, is high arousal a bad thing in sport?

Well, on the basis that arousal is really just a state of alertness or stimulation, it is neither good nor bad in itself. The way in which you *label* your arousal, however, is crucial. Put simply, anxiety is just an emotional label for a particular type of bodily experience – namely, an unpleasant state of high arousal. And so, whereas some athletes (like Tiger Woods and Dan Carter) regard rapid heart-beat, shortness of breath and butterflies in the stomach as welcome signs of being appropriately 'psyched up' or excited, others perceive exactly the same physical sensations as being unpleasant feelings of anxiety. Given this fact that you can interpret the same level of arousal in different ways, is anxiety a help or a hindrance to your performance in sport?

4. Anxiety can either help or hinder performance – depending on how you interpret it

Earlier, we explained that it is not the amount of arousal that affects your performance but the way in which you *label* such arousal that matters. In other words, the bodily symptoms of anxiety can either help or hinder athletic performance depending on how you perceive them.

Hitting the mark

One of us was once consulted by an international sprinter who complained that pre-race anxiety was beginning to impair his performance in competitive athletics. Specifically, he said that his heart used to beat so fast before a race that he felt that rival athletes might even be able to hear it or see it as they prepared on the blocks. After some observation and analysis of his pre-race routine, we discovered a simple strategy to overcome this problem. We trained the sprinter to interpret his anxiety differently by convincing him to identify his pounding heart as the key in his body's 'ignition' – we trained him to believe that when it starts to beat fast, it simply means that he's now ready and primed for an explosive start.

So, what does anxiety mean to you?

What does anxiety mean to you?

- What does the word anxiety mean to you? Do you think that it is helpful or harmful to your performance?
- On a scale of 0 (meaning 'not at all important') to 5 (meaning 'extremely important'), how important do you think that the ability to control anxiety is for successful performance in your sport?
- Do you prefer to be 'psyched up' or to be calm before a competitive event in your sport? Why? Please explain.
- What things make you anxious before a competition? How do these factors affect your performance? Explain.
- What things make you anxious during a competition? How do these factors affect your performance?
- What techniques do you use, if any, to cope with anxiety in your sport? Where did you learn these techniques?
- How would you like to react to things that make you anxious at present?

5. Anxiety affects you at different levels

Research shows that anxiety affects you at three different levels – cognitive, physical and behavioural. Let's explore each of these levels in turn. First, as we explained above, cognitive anxiety involves worrying about the outcome of some impending competitive situation. This worrying takes your mind off the job at hand and encourages you to think too far ahead (a problem that we shall deal with in Chapter 5). Next, anxiety can strike you at the physical level through increased perspiration, a pounding heart, rapid shallow breathing, clammy hands and butterflies in your stomach. Third, anxiety can affect you behaviourally by causing tense facial expressions and jerky, uncoordinated bodily movements. In sport, all three levels of the anxiety experience often occur simultaneously. So, going back to a previous example, if you're on the tee-box of the first hole in the Captain's Prize with lots of people watching you, you may worry about hitting your drive into the water, feel short of breath and experience bodily tension as you stand over the ball while preparing to play.

6. We each have our own zone of peak performance

Research on the relationship between anxiety, stress and performance in sport confirms something that many of us know informally – we are all different. Put simply, although different anxiety experiences have some common elements, we each respond to pressure situations in our own unique way. Clearly, therefore, the person who is best placed to know how you respond is – yourself. Using some of the techniques outlined in Chapter 3, you can begin to understand the level of anxiety that works best for you, and then to develop pre-match routines that ensure you can hit that mark whenever you want to do so.

Hitting the zone

Before considering some techniques that you can use to manage your anxiety, it may be worthwhile spending a few moments reflecting on the level of anxiety that seems to work best for you.

Good times, bad times

The good time

First of all, think of an occasion where you felt that you played particularly well and close to your best. This may be recently or could be any time since you started to compete. Having thought of that time, now try to remember all the circumstances surrounding the event. This should include the whole build up to the game. Were you distracted or focused in the days and weeks beforehand? Were there lots of other things on your mind? Were you generally worried or chilled? Were you angry or calm? Did you sleep well beforehand? Did you go to bed early, late or at the same time? On the day of competition, did you laze around or busy yourself? Were you deliberately thinking of the game or were other things dominating your thoughts? Did you feel lethargic or energised? Did you feel agitated or calm? Did you arrive early or late? Did you have too much time beforehand or not enough? What were the changing room and warm up routines? How did you think about the opposition? Was it an important game? Were you underdog or top dog? Were you home or away?

The bad time

Now think of an occasion where you felt that you performed particularly badly and below your expectation, and this was not because of injury or illness – you simply blobbed. Again try to remember all the circumstances leading up to and surrounding the event.

The good and the bad

Now think of all the other occasions when you either performed well or badly – and what led up to those performances. You can use all these reflections to start to build a profile of the anxiety level that works best for you. One technique is to describe your stress level like a 'stressometer' (where 0 = no stress and 100 = wired to the moon), and your goal is to put in place a regime that will allow you to keep hitting the same mark on the stressometer, your zone, time and again, whatever the occasion.

By reflecting on the differences between the way in which you felt before performances that were *successful* and those that turned out to be *unsuccessful*, you can gain important insights into your preferred pre-competition routine and your optimal arousal level. This routine should include a number of active relaxation techniques that can help you to hit the mark and stay in your zone. One such technique involves breathing slowly and deeply, lowering your shoulders to reduce bodily tension, and taking your pulse (either on your neck or wrist). When you begin to recognise what the rate of your resting pulse feels like, you can start to use mental imagery techniques (see Chapter 6) to help you to change it to the desired level.

Managing stress: Taking control

To illustrate how easy it is to manage your stress level, try closing your eyes (after reading this!) while at the same time registering your resting pulse. Now bring to mind first of all those things that are causing you the most anxiety in your life at the moment. They can be inside or away from sport but try hard to immerse yourself in these worries. As you focus your thoughts on these sources of stress you should detect your pulse rate rising. Now work hard to replace these anxious thoughts with the image of a place in the world that you find most relaxing – it could be somewhere quiet at home, in the countryside, on holiday, anywhere that you are alone, and where you feel comfortable and at ease. Try bringing to mind the sights, sounds, smells and even 'feel' of the place, and then have a single word that you can use as a cue for bringing this place to mind. As you work hard to focus on this quiet place you should detect your pulse rate starting to fall, and with practice the change can be dramatic, and quick. If at first you don't succeed then keep practising and eventually you will have a powerful self-driven stress management tool always at your disposal.

Many top athletes have intuitively developed similar psychological techniques for making sure that they perform to the best of their ability. For example, back in the 1970s, much to the annoyance of many of his team-mates, one of the most talented rugby players of all time, the Welsh outside-half Barry John, regularly detached himself from the rest of the team during frantic pre-match build-ups by lying down quietly in the corner of the changing room. What on earth was he doing? Hitting his zone.

What makes you feel anxious in sport?

As you would expect from such a complex psychological and physical response, nervousness in sport is caused by many factors. Here are some of the most important ones.

Barry John (Courtesy of Inpho Photography)

1. How much importance you attach to the game

The more importance that you attach to a sporting encounter, the more nervous you are inclined to become beforehand. Playing a friendly match is usually less stressful than playing a competitive match because there is little at stake besides your pride. But even a friendly match can make you feel anxious if you are aware that you are being watched by a coach or family member whom you are trying hard to impress. Clearly, the way in which you *perceive* a match is at least as significant as its competitive status.

2. Your expectations

Thinking and anxiety are strongly related. So, if you set impossibly high standards for your performance and judge yourself harshly for failing to achieve them, you will tend to become anxious – and may even give up – whenever you encounter setbacks in sport. For example, Ronnie O'Sullivan, the mercurial snooker player, made history in 2006 when he conceded a quarter-final match against Stephen Hendry at 1-4 down in a 'first to 9' frame match. Afterwards, he blamed his sudden exit on his apparent failure to satisfy his own high standards:

> 'Anyone who knows me knows I'm a perfectionist when it comes to my game and today I got so annoyed with myself that I lost my patience and walked away from a game that, with hindsight, I should have continued.'[9]

To counteract the perils of perfectionism, you need to challenge your expectations for your sporting performances. As a first step in this process, try the exercise in the box below.

Turning pressure into challenge

This exercise shows you how to use a technique called cognitive restructuring to turn a pressure situation into a manageable challenge. To begin, think of a situation that usually makes you feel anxious. Now, describe this by finishing the following sentence:

'I hate the pressure of . . .' .

Fill in the missing words with reference to the pressure situation you have experienced. For example, you might write down 'I hate the pressure of taking a short putt when a lot depends on it'.

Now, think of this pressure situation again. This time, however, I would like you to restructure it in your head so that you think about it differently.

'I love the challenge of . . .'.

Please note, you're not allowed to simply repeat what you wrote before. You can't just say 'I love the challenge of taking a short putt when a lot depends on it'. Instead, pick something else to focus on in that pressure situation besides the fear of making mistakes. As we shall see in Chapter 6, the secret of maintaining your focus under pressure is to concentrate on something that is specific, relevant and under your own control. Usually, that means concentrating on some aspect of your preparation for the feared situation – you could write 'I love the challenge of keeping my head steady every time I putt – no matter what the score is or who I'm playing against'. Notice how restructuring a situation can make you feel and think differently about it. You no longer see it as something to fear but as something that challenges your skills.

3. Fear of failure

As Chapter 2 makes clear, every competitor suffers fear of failure from time to time, even those at the top of their sport. For example, Ronaldo, the former Brazilian soccer star, experienced a severe attack of nerves on the night before his team lost to France in the 1998 World Cup final. According to his team-mate, Roberto Carlos, this nervousness was triggered by a fear of failure:

> 'He was scared about what lay ahead. The pressure had got to him and he couldn't stop crying.'[10]

One way of overcoming this type of fear is to make a list of two or three jobs that are under your control in the competitive situation and then try to 'see' and 'feel' yourself performing each of these tasks smoothly (see also Chapter 6). The idea here is that as your mind can think of only one thing at a time, you're replacing a negative thought with a positive imagined action.

4. Lack of confidence

If you have little confidence in your own abilities, you are likely to experience high levels of anxiety in competitive situations. Of course, the obvious solution to this problem lies in practising harder. This idea was expressed by the great golfer Sam Snead when advising players who admitted to being afraid of certain shots:

> 'If you're scared of your 7-iron, go and practise it!'

Having explained the nature and causes of anxiety, let's explore now what we know about how nervousness can actually affect your performance.

How does anxiety affect performance?

Earlier, we suggested that the ability to regulate your level of arousal is a vital mental skill in competitive sport. Not surprisingly, many athletes and coaches have developed techniques designed either to energise themselves when they feel flat or to lower their arousal levels when they feel too agitated before a match. For example, if you're a wrestler, a weight-lifter or are involved in contact sports where high levels of physiological arousal may be linked to success, it may be important to develop 'psych up' strategies such as listening to inspirational music in the hours or minutes before a competitive event. Other sports may require much lower levels of arousal, and here the choice of music may be quite different. Ideally, you should choose music not to *match* your mood – but to *change* it in a desired direction. Using this principle, many athletes use their iPods to create personalised medleys of tunes to generate the right mood for their best performance.

Of course, music is not the only psych up or psych down strategy used in sport. Curiously, some coaches believe that if players are made angry before they compete, their performance will be improved. One advocate of this rather bizarre theory was Laurent Seigne, a French rugby coach who is reported to have punched members of his team, Brive, before a match in order to raise their game.[11] Arousal regulation strategies are also used in precision sports such as golf and snooker where performers need to calm down in order to play well. For example, the golfer Philip Walton used deep breathing to lower his arousal level on the 18th green when defeating Jay Haas (USA) in the 1995 Ryder Cup:

> *'What saved me was . . . something I learned . . . about how to breathe properly in a stressful situation. You do it from your belly not high up in your chest.'*[12]

Of course, arousal regulation strategies are not always effective. This leads us to one of the biggest problems of nervousness in sport – 'choking' under pressure.

Choking under pressure

Earlier in the chapter, we explained that 'anxiety' and 'choking' are closely related terms. In sport, 'choking' under pressure occurs when an athlete's normally expert level of performance deteriorates suddenly and significantly under conditions of perceived pressure. As you might expect, nervousness has prompted some dramatic collapses in athletic performance – especially in precision sports like golf and tennis. For example, golfer Jean van de Velde infamously squandered his chance of winning the 1999 Open Championship at Carnoustie, when, leading the field by 3 strokes, he shot a triple-bogey on the final hole (and lost the resulting play-off for the title). Similarly, when Jana Novotna (the Czech Republic) was leading Steffi Graf (Germany) 4–3 in the third set of the 1993 Wimbledon Ladies' Singles final, she became so anxious that she served three *consecutive* double-faults. Not surprisingly, she lost the match.

Jana Novotna (Courtesy of Inpho Photography)

Choking in sport is so widespread that it is known by a variety of terms such as the 'yips' in golf, 'icing' or 'bricking' in basketball, 'dartitis' in darts and 'bottling' in soccer. As Tom Watson (the former world number 1 golfer) once remarked wryly,

> *'We all choke. You just try to choke last!'*[13]

But what exactly are the symptoms of choking and what causes this problem?

What is choking?

As we explained earlier, choking involves the sudden deterioration of normally expert skills under pressure. Perhaps the most fascinating aspect of this state of mind is not that it leads to poor performance – but that it seems to stem from a motivational paradox. Specifically, the more effort that you put into your performance when you're extremely anxious, the worse it gets. In other words, choking under pressure occurs ironically because you're trying *too hard* to perform well.

The symptoms of choking in sport are broadly similar to those experienced when you're highly aroused physiologically. They include tense muscles, shaky limbs, rapid heart and pulse rates, shortness of breath, butterflies in the stomach, 'racing' thoughts and feelings of panic. In addition, choking often involves the anxious struggle to complete a stroke or movement that you can normally perform effortlessly. This unpleasant feeling of 'paralysis by analysis' is well captured by the renowned former golfer and commentator Peter Alliss:

> *'I stood over the ball, lining up the putt and suddenly I was gripped by negative thoughts. I couldn't visualise the ball going in. I was frightened of failure and I could barely draw back the putter to make contact with the ball.'*[14]

Likewise, pitchers in baseball or bowlers in cricket who suffer from anxiety attacks suddenly feel as if they cannot release the ball. On one occasion Phil Edmonds, the former England cricket bowler, was so badly afflicted with anxiety that he ended up standing in the crease and lobbing the ball at the batter's end.

Choking reactions to pressure may also be characterised by a tiny muscular spasm that occurs just as the stroke is about to be executed. The late Scottish darts player Jocky Wilson was legendary in his sport for the various tics and twitches that came to characterise his unique throwing action – especially in the latter stages of his career.

What causes choking?

Many psychologists regard choking as an anxiety-based, concentration lapse rather than a personality weakness. This distinction is important because it suggests that *anyone* can choke under pressure if they pay attention to the 'wrong' target – anything which is outside their control or which is irrelevant to the task at hand (see also Chapter 5). For example, if nervousness makes you think too much about yourself or the importance of the event in which you are competing, your performance will probably deteriorate. Psychologically, what's happening here is that you're 'reinvesting'[15] or trying to consciously control skills that are better performed automatically. Research shows that in such circumstances, your skills will tend to unravel.

Having explored the symptoms and causes of choking, let's now show you how to cope with pressure situations in sport.

Coping with pressure: The eight-point plan

Before we explain our eight-point plan for coping with pressure, we need to distinguish between *pressure situations* and *pressure reactions* in sport. Briefly, whereas pressure situations are adverse circumstances that can be described objectively (e.g., playing in a team that is trailing 1-0 in a match with three minutes left to play), pressure reactions (i.e., how one interprets and responds to the circumstances in question) are largely subjective. But because 'pressure' is a *perception* not a fact, you don't have to experience anxiety in pressure situations. In fact, you could look at them as exciting opportunities to test yourself against others. With this idea in mind, here is our eight-point plan for coping with pressure situations.

1. Restructure the pressure situation in your mind

People experience anxiety whenever they believe that a current or impending situation threatens them in some way. For example, you may be nervous of making a mistake in an important football match in case you let your team-mates down. This fear can haunt even the best athletes in the world. Thus Victoria Pendleton, a British Olympic gold medallist and world champion in cycling, admitted that,

'. . . feeling I have let people down is my biggest battle in life . . . and when I do, I feel such a failure.'[16]

More generally, whenever there is a discrepancy between what you *think* you can do (i.e., your assessment of your own abilities) and what you believe you are *expected* to do (i.e., what you perceive as the demands of the situation), you put yourself under pressure. Psychologically, therefore, pressure is a subjective interpretation of certain objective circumstances (the 'pressure situation').

Another point to note is that although you cannot change a pressure situation, you *can* definitely change your reaction to it using a technique called 'restructuring' or changing the way you look at a situation. The idea here is that by restructuring a pressure situation in your mind, you can learn to interpret it as a challenge to your abilities rather than as a threat to your well-being. To illustrate, consider how Jack Nicklaus, who is statistically the greatest golfer ever by virtue of his 18 major tournament victories, distinguished between feeling nervous and feeling excited:

> *'Sure, you're nervous, but that's the difference between being able to win and not being able to win. And that's the fun of it, to put yourself in the position of being nervous, being excited. I never look on it as pressure. I look on it as fun and excitement. That's why you're doing it.'*[17]

Jack Nicklaus (Courtesy of Inpho Photography)

Good examples of restructuring in action come from multiple Olympic gold medallists Michael Phelps (swimming) and Usain Bolt (sprinting). According to Phelps:

> *'You can look at pressure in two different ways. It's either going to hurt you or help you. I see it as something that helps me. If there's pressure on me or someone thinks I can't do something, it's going to make me work even harder.'*[18]

A different kind of restructuring was used by Usain Bolt during the 2012 Olympic Games in London. Bothered by self-doubt about his relatively slow starts in races, Bolt revealed that his coach had solved the problem by convincing him to

> *'stop worrying about the start because the best part of your race is at the end!'*[19]

To explore this skill of cognitive restructuring for yourself, try the exercise below.

Are you being too hard on yourself?

What are your expectations of yourself when you compete? To answer this question, ask yourself if any of the following thoughts seem familiar to you before or during a game.

- 'I must defeat my opponent easily in this game: If I don't, I might as well give up' (black-and-white thinking).
- 'If I miss this chance, I'm definitely going to struggle for the rest of the game' ('fortune telling' or predicting the future).
- 'I/we always play badly when the weather is like this' (over-generalisation).
- 'I know that "X" blamed me for a mistake even though s/he didn't say anything to me at the time' (mind-reading).

A common theme in each of these statements is that they confuse *facts* with *interpretations*. In each case, you have put yourself under pressure by making a false assumption about your game or by jumping to premature or invalid conclusions. The solution to this problem is to stop being so hard on yourself by learning to look at things differently. For example, clear your mind before you play and try to eliminate global words like 'should', 'must' and 'never' from your vocabulary.

Having explained how to restructure pressure situations as challenges, the next step is to explore some practical techniques for reducing anxiety.

2. Learn to understand what your body is telling you

Despite their talent and experience, many top sportspeople still have a poor understanding of what their body is telling them when they are anxious. Remember, anxiety is not necessarily a bad thing but merely a sign that you *care* about what you're doing and what's at stake. So, the first step in coping with anxiety is to become tuned in to what it really means.

3. Use physical relaxation techniques

In the heat of competition, athletes tend to speed up their behaviour. This is not surprising in view of the 'fight or flight' reaction that we discussed earlier in the chapter. If you have experienced this problem, the obvious solution is to make a deliberate effort to slow down and relax whenever tension strikes. Of course, this advice must be tailored to the demands of the particular sport that you're playing. In fact, the feasibility of using physical relaxation techniques such as progressive muscular relaxation depends heavily on the amount of 'break time' offered by the sport in question. For example, in stop-start untimed sports like golf or tennis, there are moments where it may be possible to lower your shoulders, flap out the tension from your arms and engage in deep breathing exercises. Centring is a technique used in many sports, and can easily be adapted to meet the particular requirements of your own sport. For example, in rugby union, a hooker could easily introduce centring into the line-out pre-throw routine to ensure there is no tension in the upper body and throwing arm.

Centring

At any stage during play it may be necessary to stop, take stock and take control. Centring enables you quickly and simply to counteract some of the changes associated with physical tension and associated loss of control. All it takes is a few seconds to 'calm yourself down' to a point where you regain the capacity to assess the situation accurately and then direct your concentration in appropriate ways.

1. Stand with your feet shoulder-width apart and knees slightly bent. Your weight should be evenly balanced between your two feet. The bend in your knees is important and should result in you being able to feel the tension in the muscles in the calves and thighs. The flexing counteracts a natural tendency to lock knees when you become tense.
2. Now, consciously relax your neck and shoulder muscles. Check this by making slight movements with your head and arms (see that they are loose and relaxed).

3. Your mouth should be open slightly to reduce tension in jaw muscles.
4. Breathe in from your diaphragm, down to your abdomen. Inhale slowly and, as you do, attend to two cues. First, notice that you extend your stomach as you breathe. Next, consciously maintain relaxation in your chest and shoulders. This helps you avoid allowing your chest to expand and shoulders to rise, thus increasing upper body tension. It also counters a tendency to tense your neck and shoulder muscles.
5. As you breathe out slowly, notice the feelings in your abdomen and your stomach muscles relaxing. Consciously let your knees bend slightly, attending to increased feelings of heaviness as your body presses down towards the ground. The exhalation counteracts the natural lifting associated with breathing in and the body does begin to feel more steady.
6. As you have attended to the relaxing physical cues you have simultaneously stopped attending to the things that were causing you to lose control. Now you should have recovered enough composure to deal in a constructive way with the situation you face.

To facilitate centring, some professional tennis players use a relaxation strategy whereby they visualise an imaginary area (usually located behind the baseline of a tennis court) which serves as a relaxation zone where they can switch off mentally during breaks in play (see also Chapter 6).

If you feel that you may benefit from relaxation skills, try using the following script. It can be used as a general lifestyle tool or perhaps to create the right environment for a good night's sleep. Closer to competition, it may help you to create the right emotional environment during your pre-competition routine.

Self-directed relaxation

Lie down on a flat, firm surface.

Close your eyes and adjust your position so you are stretched out making maximum contact with the ground. Raise and lower your head to stretch your neck, making sure your neck is not tilted backwards. Flatten your back and push away with your heels to stretch your legs. Take a deep breath and let it out slowly. Feel the weight of your body on the floor, take another deep breath and let the floor support your full weight. Take a deep breath and slowly breathe out. Think of the word 'relax' then pause. Breathe in deeply . . . breathe out slowly . . . breathe in deeply . . . breathe out slowly.

Now focus all your attention on your head. Feel any tension in your forehead. Just relax the tension in your forehead. Relax . . . (pause). Relax even deeper . . . and deeper . . . and deeper.

Feel any tension in your jaw. Just relax the tension in these muscles. Feel the tension flow away. Breathe in deeply . . . breathe out slowly.

Feel the relaxation in your facial muscles. Relax . . . then pause. Breathe in deeply . . . breathe out slowly (pause). Relax even deeper . . . and deeper . . . and deeper.

Now feel any tension in your arms, forearms and hands. Just relax the muscles in your arms. Relax . . . (pause).

Feel any tension in your hands, fingers or arms, and just relax the tension in these muscles. Feel the tension flow away from your body. Breathe in deeply . . . breathe out slowly.

Feel the relaxation in your arms and hands. Relax . . . (pause). Breathe in deeply . . . breathe out slowly (pause). Relax even deeper . . . and deeper . . . and deeper.

Now focus your attention on your neck and upper back. Feel any tension in the muscles of your neck and upper back. Just relax the tension in these muscles. Relax . . . (pause). See the tension flow out of your body. Breathe in deeply . . . breathe out slowly. Feel the relaxation in these muscles. Relax . . . (pause). Breathe in deeply . . . breathe out slowly (pause). Relax even deeper . . . and deeper . . . and deeper.

Remember to keep your facial muscles relaxed. Keep your arms and hand muscles relaxed. And keep your neck and upper back muscles relaxed. Keep all these muscles relaxed. Inhale deeply . . . exhale slowly. Feel the relaxation in all these muscles. Feel the relaxation even deeper . . . and deeper . . . and deeper.

Now feel any tension in your lower back and stomach muscles. Focus all your attention on these muscles and get them to relax. Relax these muscles fully. Feel the tension flow away. Breathe in deeply . . . breathe out slowly. Feel the relaxation in your lower back and stomach muscles. Relax . . . (pause). Breathe in deeply . . . breathe out slowly (pause). Relax even deeper . . . and deeper . . . and deeper.

Now feel any tension in your upper legs, both the front and back. Focus all your attention on these muscles and get them to relax. Relax these muscles fully. Feel the tension flow away. Breathe in deeply . . . breathe out slowly. Feel the relaxation in your upper legs. Relax . . . (pause). Breathe in deeply . . . breathe out slowly (pause). Relax even deeper . . . and deeper . . . and deeper.

Remember to keep your facial muscles relaxed. Keep your lower back and stomach muscles relaxed. And keep your upper leg muscles relaxed – keep all these muscles relaxed. Breathe in deeply . . . breathe out slowly. Feel the relaxation in all these muscles. Feel the relaxation even deeper . . . and deeper . . . and deeper.

Now feel any tension in your lower legs and your feet. Focus all your attention on these muscles and ask them to relax. Relax these muscles fully. Feel the tension flow away. Breathe in deeply . . . breathe out slowly. Feel the relaxation in your lower legs and feet. Relax . . . (pause). Breathe in deeply . . . breathe out slowly (pause). Relax even deeper.

With practice, you can gradually combine the muscle groups together into larger units (e.g., head, neck and arms; torso; lower body) until the whole exercise takes only a few seconds.

The golfer Sam Torrance used a similar procedure prior to almost every major tournament that he played in – only in his case he wasn't lying on the floor, he was sitting on the toilet, and he knew he had reached the required state when the cigarette he was invariably holding fell to the floor!

4. Give yourself specific instructions

As we indicated earlier, anxiety is unhelpful because it makes us focus on what might go *wrong* (the outcome) rather than on what we actually have to do (the challenge facing us). Therefore, a useful way to counteract pressure in a competition is to ask yourself: 'What exactly do I have to do right now?' By focusing on what you have to do, you can learn to avoid the trap of confusing the facts of the situation (e.g., 'we're 1-0 down with ten minutes to go') with an anxious interpretation of those facts ('it's no use, we're going to lose'). Based on this idea, a useful practical tip for coping with pressure is to give yourself specific commands (e.g., you could say 'go cross court' to yourself when preparing to receive a serve in tennis).

5. Use a pre-performance routine

Another good way to deal with anxiety is to use 'pre-performance routines', or systematic sequences of preparatory thoughts and actions before important skills (e.g., golf putts, penalty kicks; see also Chapter 5). Routines are valuable because they take you from thinking about something to doing it. By encouraging you to take one step at a time instead of worrying about what might happen in the future, they help you to focus on the present rather than thinking of the past. Also, as routines teach you to focus only on what you can control, they cocoon you against the adverse effects of anxiety.

To illustrate a routine in action, a Gaelic footballer that we worked with rediscovered his set piece kicking ability by developing a pre-performance routine that he had used in his youth. It involved setting the ball on the ground, glancing at the target, looking at the ball, taking five steps backwards, three to the side, looking at the ball again, looking at the posts – and then singing to himself 'We built this city on rock and roll' as he ran up to kick the ball over the black spot!

Bullseye!

In a high precision sport such as archery, it is vital that the flow or rhythm of each shot is constant but is controlled by a measured routine. Here is an example of one routine used in archery. The routine begins the moment the arrow is taken from the quiver. This also acts as the signal to stop the evaluation of the previous shot and focus all attention on the next.

1. **Check** – before loading the bow, a quick check that physically things feel right – this could include a breathing exercise. Only proceed when things feel right and have the courage to begin again if they don't.
2. **Load** – the bow faces the ground while the arrow is loaded and the required tension is applied to the bowstring.
3. **Spot** – the bow is slowly raised until the arrow points to a pre-designated spot on the adjacent wall.
4. **Stance** – a quick check that the whole body stance is good.
5. **Swing** – the archer rotates through 90 degrees until the arrow points to the target.
6. **Head** – checking that the correct head position is adopted.
7. **Gold** – attention focuses on the gold spot at the centre of the target.
8. **Squeeze** – the release mechanism is activated and the arrow flies.

Over time the script could be shortened but should always be there, in both training and competition. To make sure the correct tempo or timing is maintained, the words could even be set to a rhythm or song.

6. Think constructively and encourage yourself

When you are anxious, your 'self-talk' (i.e., what you say to yourself silently inside your head) tends to becomes hostile and sarcastic. Although such frustration is understandable, it usually makes the situation worse. So when you're talking to yourself, try to encourage yourself for your effort or to instruct yourself on what to do next. For example, if you're an anxious table tennis player, you might say to yourself 'Come on, this point now' (encouragement); 'Attack the backhand' (guidance).

7. Get used to pressure situations by training in them

One of the best ways to develop mental toughness is to practise under simulated pressure situations in training. Preparing for the worst can help you to do your best. For example, as part of their training for gold-medal success in the 1988 Olympics, the Australian women's hockey team practised under adversity such as gamesmanship (especially verbal 'sledging' or name-calling) and bad umpiring decisions.

8. Control your body language

If you are nervous, your shoulders will tighten up, your breathing will increase and your body movements will tend to become jerky. By making an effort to lower your shoulders, breathe more deeply and slow down, you'll not only conquer your feelings of anxiety but you'll also send a more confident image to your opponents.

The last word

In this chapter, we have shown you that you can learn to cope with pressure situations by using a variety of psychological strategies. First, remember that pressure lies in the eye of the beholder. So, you must learn to cognitively restructure competitive events as *opportunities* to display your talents (the challenge response) rather than as potential sources of failure (the fear response). Second, you have to learn for yourself what level of stress works best for you and which combination of practical strategies can help bring you to your 'zone' before a competitive game. One way of doing this is to use simulation training and mental rehearsal to prepare yourself for the challenges that lie ahead. Third, you can benefit from using self-talk techniques to guide yourself through pressure situations. Finally, when anxiety strikes, you must be prepared to deepen your routines and to use physical relaxation procedures in accordance with the structure of your sport. In other words, when the going gets tough, the tough keep doing what got them there in the first place.

Go unconscious!
Darren Clarke. Courtesy of Inpho Photography. See page 5

'It's down to their mentality.'
Brian O'Driscoll. Courtesy of Inpho Photography. See page 12

'I believe in myself.'
Dai Greene. Courtesy of Inpho Photography. See page 12

'I am making mistakes which, hopefully, I am learning from.'
Rory McIlroy. Courtesy of Inpho Photography. See page 15

Still running after all these years.
Fauja Singh. Courtesy of Inpho Photography. See page 20

No psychology!
Leinster winning 2011 European Heineken Cup. Courtesy of Inpho Photography. See page 21

The siege mentality!
Alex Ferguson. Courtesy of Inpho Photography. See page 22

'It will mean something very special if I reach that goal.'
Michael Phelps. Courtesy of Inpho Photography. See page 42

'Feeling I have let people down is my biggest battle in life.'
Victoria Pendleton. Courtesy of Inpho Photography. See pages 62–63

The scream – fair or foul?
Maria Sharapova. Courtesy of Inpho Photography. See page 78

'Even when they trailed, even when they doubted, they remained faithful to their philosophy, their identity.'
Barcelona FC. Courtesy of Inpho Photography. See page 135

The dream team?
Brian Clough and Peter Taylor. Courtesy of Inpho Photography. See page 149

A gang culture? Far from it!
'The Crazy Gang' (Wimbledon FC). Courtesy of Inpho Photography. See page 133

'Welcome to a club whose idea of perfect harmony is to ensure players compete from dawn to dusk.'
Leicester Tigers. Courtesy of Inpho Photography. See page 132

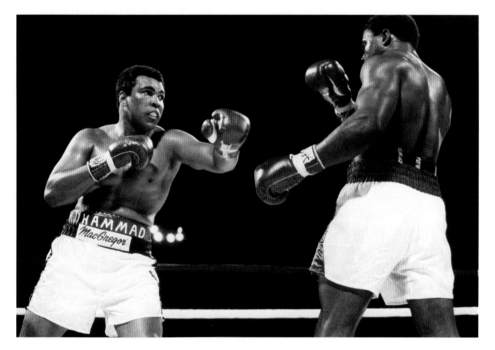

Growing stronger through adversity.
Muhammad Ali. Courtesy of Inpho Photography. See page 110

'A little bit of visualisation work.'
Jenson Button. Courtesy of Inpho Photography. See page 89

'Reaching greatness requires falling off the edge a load of times and having the courage to get back up and get on with it.'
Pádraig Harrington. Courtesy of Inpho Photography. See page 108

'Because I choose.'
Tony McCoy. Courtesy of Inpho Photography. See page 164

'I still want more.'
Mark Cavendish. Courtesy of Inpho Photography. See page 167

5 Staying focused

'Come on, concentrate!' Has a coach or team-mate ever shouted this instruction at you during a game? If so, you probably noticed that it's rarely successful for a rather obvious reason. The problem is that although a request to 'concentrate' may encourage you to try harder, it fails to tell you *exactly* what to focus on. The lesson from this everyday experience is clear. Asking someone to concentrate is meaningless unless the request is linked to a specific action – preferably one that's immediate and under your control. For example, if a fellow defender in soccer urges you to 'hold the line', then you know exactly what you have to do. Here, it is easy to concentrate because your mind has a definite behavioural target.

Unfortunately, it's very difficult to stay focused for long in competitive sport – partly because of the way our minds evolved and partly because of the number and variety of distractions that we encounter there. To explain, for our ancestors, the experience of becoming absorbed in a task was potentially dangerous because it made them vulnerable to attacks from predators. Therefore, distractibility is 'hard-wired' into our minds because it was adaptive in the past to constantly monitor our environment for signs of threat. Compounding this problem is the fact that competitive sport generates a multitude of distractions for us. For example, lapses of concentration can occur as a result of bad refereeing decisions, opponents' gamesmanship and even weather conditions on the big day. To make matters worse, you can even distract *yourself* by the way in which you think. Interestingly, this problem applies to performers at all levels of sport – even to elite athletes. In this regard, imagine the jumble of thoughts that must have gone through the mind of golfer Paul McGinley as he faced a tricky six-foot putt to win the 2002 Ryder Cup for Europe against the USA at the Belfry. Should he concentrate on the ball, on the hole, on some technical aspect of his stroke action, or, simply, on *not* missing the putt because of its importance to his team? Fortunately for Europe, McGinley not only chose the right target to focus on – the line of his putt – but by holing out, he helped his team to victory.

Although winning rarely comes down to just one shot, it is definitely made more likely by good decision making. That's where McGinley showed wonderful mental strength because his choice of target involved a specific action that was completely under his control. As he revealed afterwards,

'At no time did I even consider the mechanics of the stroke. Of course, I knew what the putt meant and what it was for, but I became absorbed in the line of the putt. I could see it exactly from beginning to end. My only job at that moment in time was to set the ball off on the line that I had chosen. That was the only thing I could control.'[1]

Clearly, although sport is played with the body, it is *won* in the mind. But what exactly is this winning mental skill called 'focus' or 'concentration'? Why do we lose it so easily? What sort of distractions do we face in sport and what is the best way to deal with them? What are the building blocks of effective concentration? Perhaps most importantly, what practical techniques can you use to improve your concentration skills in sport? The purpose of this chapter is to answer these and other relevant questions. But before we begin, let's explore the concentration skills of athletes who produce winning performances in sport.

What winners do

Let's begin this section by analysing Paul McGinley's quotation above. It's fascinating psychologically for four reasons. First, it highlights the fact that in order to focus properly, you have to have a clear goal (in his case, to sink a putt) and you need to focus on a job that's under your control – to guide the ball down the line towards the hole. Second, it shows us that when you're under pressure, it is dangerous to think too much about the mechanics of your skills. Otherwise, you could experience paralysis by analysis (see Chapter 4). Third, McGinley's remarks are interesting because they suggest that in order to perform to the best of your ability, you have to *clear* your mind of all distracting thoughts. This 'de-cluttering' principle is echoed by other winners in sport. For example, Michael Johnson (three times an Olympic gold medallist in the 400m, and nine times a world athletics gold medallist) deliberately cleared his mind before every race so that he ended up with only one thought:

'I have learned to cut out all the unnecessary thoughts . . . on the track. I simply concentrate. I concentrate on the tangible – on the track, on the race, on the blocks, on the things I have to do. The crowd fades away and the other athletes disappear and now it's just me and this one lane.'[2]

Unfortunately, this skill of clearing your mind doesn't come naturally to most people, even top athletes. That's why golfers often use their caddies as sounding boards – to stop themselves from thinking too much. For example, Rory McIlroy, a two-time golf major winner and winner of the Dubai World Championship in 2012, admitted that

'Having a conversation about something completely different is probably the best thing for me as it takes my mind off it and stops me getting too involved in what I'm doing.'[3]

Michael Johnson (Courtesy of Inpho Photography)

The final learning point from McGinley's quotation is that when two opponents are evenly matched, victory is usually achieved by the one who is better able to focus on the task at hand while ignoring distractions. This idea brings us to the main theme of this chapter. What separates the winners from the losers in sport is the ability to stay in the present and to focus on what you can do *right now* rather than speculating about what might happen in the future. It is precisely this skill that helped Bradley Wiggins to become the first cyclist to win both the Tour de France and an Olympic gold medal in the same year (2012):

> 'I never think too far ahead. How can you think three days ahead when you've got two days in-between? . . . I'll just keep going, day by day.'[4]

Having learned some valuable lessons about effective focusing from winners in sport, let's explore what the term 'concentration' really means.

What is concentration or 'focus'?

In sport psychology, the term 'concentration' or 'focus' usually means paying attention to what is most important in any situation while ignoring distractions. But it has two other meanings. Let's explore these various meanings now.

Selective attention

To begin with, concentration means focused or 'selective' attention – your ability to 'zoom in' on relevant information while ignoring potential distractions. To illustrate, if you are a goalkeeper in hockey waiting for a penalty corner from the opposing team, you must be able to focus selectively on the ball while ignoring the constant movement of the players in the penalty area.

Conscious attention

Second, 'concentration' can mean conscious attention or making a deliberate decision to invest mental effort in something that is important to you. For example, at a team talk before an important match you will probably make a big effort to listen carefully to your coach's instructions. By contrast, you may find that your mind wanders easily when you're in a training session.

Unconscious attention

Finally, concentration can mean unconscious attention which concerns your ability to perform two or more skills at the same time. Such mental time-sharing occurs when one of the skills you're performing is so highly practised that it's become automatic. For example, if you're a skilled basketball player, you should be able to dribble with the ball while simultaneously scanning the court for a team-mate who's in a good position to receive a pass.

Although all three aspects of concentration are important in sport, we're going to deal with the first and second of these processes in this chapter because to concentrate properly, you have to *decide* to focus (conscious attention) and then pay attention to the most important aspects of the situation while ignoring less important ones (selective attention). Let's explore these processes more deeply now.

Your mental spotlight

Concentration is best understood as a mental spotlight that you shine at things that interest you. In some ways, it is like the head-mounted torches that miners, divers and potholers wear in dark environments. Wherever they look, their target is illuminated. So, you're in control of your own concentration beam. When you shine your mental spotlight at a target in the world around you (e.g., as you look at your team-mates before the start of a match) you have an *external* focus of attention at that moment. But when you concentrate on your own feelings or bodily processes (e.g., in listening to your heart pounding with excitement before kick-off), you have switched to an *internal* focus of attention. Typically, in team sports, an external focus of attention is required when you're trying to 'read' a game, pass to a team-mate or mark an opponent. By contrast, an internal focus is needed when you're devising a game plan or rehearsing a skill in your mind's eye before you perform it (see also Chapter 6).

Interestingly, your mental spotlight also has an adjustable beam – it can be broad or narrow. Whereas a *broad* focus allows you to absorb lots of information rapidly (e.g., before you take a throw-in in soccer, you quickly check out your

In the spotlight

team-mates' positions), a *narrow* focus ensures that you have only one thing on your mind (e.g., deciding which side of the goal to aim at before you take a penalty kick).

Combining these ideas about the direction and width of your concentration beam, your focus at any given time falls into one of four different categories – broad external, broad internal, narrow external or narrow internal. Of course, whether the focus you've chosen is *appropriate* for the skill that you're performing is a very different question. As we learned in Chapter 4, thinking too much about your skills can cause you to freeze (paralysis by analysis). Likewise, shining your spotlight on yourself is not a good idea as it makes you self-conscious and worried about making mistakes. And focusing on what might happen in the future is also counter-productive as it encourages you to think too far ahead. We'll come back to these examples of focusing on the wrong target when we explore how easy it is to lose your concentration in sport.

Where is your spotlight shining right now?

As we have just explained, your mind is always focused on a target – whether or not it's appropriate to the job that you're doing. Hopefully, you're concentrating on the words on this page right now *but* if your mind is elsewhere, you won't even notice this sentence (or deliberate spelling mistake)! Anyway, having introduced the idea that there are different *types* of focus, let's outline what we know about them.

The four types of focus

- **A broad external focus**

  It involves the ability to read a game and quickly assess a situation for relevant information. For example, a good midfield player must be able to quickly weigh up the best passing options available to him or her having won a tackle. Peripheral awareness is the key here (especially in team sports) and involves the ability to integrate many different observations at a glance (e.g., experienced players can rapidly assess the position of team-mates and the formation of opposing players).

- **A narrow external focus**

  This type of focus is required whenever an athlete locks onto a specific target in the surrounding environment. For example, when a rugby full-back attempts a catch, s/he must focus solely on the dropping ball and ignore in-rushing opponents. Likewise, a pistol shooter has to focus on the 'bull's eye' before s/he presses the trigger.

- **A broad internal focus**

  This focus is called upon when you're developing a tactical plan for a forthcoming match. This plan might require you to analyse your opponents' strengths and weaknesses.

- **A narrow internal focus**

  This type of focus is necessary when your mind has to concentrate on a single thought or idea such as your stride or breathing as you run a marathon. Interestingly, when you're nervous, you tend to adopt this type of focus – but the target is invariably unhelpful to the action (e.g., 'I'll never be able to keep up this pace' or 'I'm playing very badly at present').

At this stage, let's see if you can come up with some examples from your own sport of the four different types of focus that we've just described.

Focusing

Every sport places concentration demands on its performers. Using the sport that you know best, try to identify the specific skills that go with each of the following types of focus.

A broad external focus?
A narrow external focus?
A broad internal focus?
A narrow internal focus?

Deceiving your opponents by diverting their spotlight

Research shows that our concentration system is very limited – we can focus on only one target at a time. Not surprisingly, this principle is often exploited by skilful athletes who try to deceive their opponents by tricking them into shining their spotlight on the *wrong* target. For example, basketball and soccer players sometimes make a 'blind' or 'no look' pass where they *look* in one direction but pass the ball to a team-mate in a *different* direction. This trick was popularised by Michael Jordan (basketball) and Ronaldinho (soccer). Incidentally, attentional diversion strategies are also used widely by stage magicians to ensure that the audience focuses on the *effects* of a trick rather than on how it is actually achieved.

'Losing' concentration: Fact or fiction?

Have you ever had the experience of suddenly discovering that you've been reading the same sentence in a book over and over again without any comprehension because your mind was 'miles away'? If so, then you have first hand experience of losing your concentration. But is concentration ever really 'lost'? While you were reading, what probably happened was that you distracted yourself by allowing a thought or daydream to become the target of your mental spotlight. So, concentration is never lost – but merely *re-directed* at some target that is irrelevant to the task at hand. With this idea in mind, let's explore the main distractions that divert our focus in sport situations.

Distractions

Although distractions come in all shapes and sizes, they can be divided into two main categories based on their origin – external and internal.

External distractions are environmental factors that divert your concentration away from its intended target. By contrast, internal distractions include a vast array of your thoughts, feelings and/or bodily sensations (e.g., pain, fatigue) that can disrupt your attempt to concentrate on the job at hand. Let's explore these two categories in more detail now.

External distractions	Internal distractions
Crowd noise/spectator behaviour	Thinking too far ahead
Weather conditions/playing surface	Reflecting on how you are feeling
Gamesmanship by opponents	Worrying about others' reactions

External distractions

Typical external distractions include factors such as crowd and/or photographer noise, spectator behaviour, weather conditions, unpredictable playing surfaces and gamesmanship by opponents. For example, in soccer, teams visiting the Turkish football club, Galatasaray, in the Ali Sami Yen stadium in Istanbul, have complained of being greeted by hostile supporters letting off fireworks and waving threatening banners bearing such messages as 'Welcome to hell!' Not surprisingly, these intimidating gestures make it difficult for visiting teams to focus properly before and during matches. Fans have distracted athletes more directly as well. For example, when Roger Federer played Robin Soderling in the 2009 French Open tennis final, a man jumped onto the court and handed him a hat to wear. Clearly rattled by this distraction, Federer lost the next three points, admitting afterwards that, 'it definitely threw me out of my rhythm.'[5] Fortunately for Federer, he regained his focus and won the match. Weather conditions can also be distracting. For instance, if you're a golfer, playing on links courses can be difficult because of unpredictable gusts of wind blowing in from the sea.

Another classic external distraction is gamesmanship by opponents. This practice is widespread in football, cricket, golf, tennis and snooker. For example, at corner-kicks in football, the opposing team's forwards often stand in front of the goalkeeper as a distraction ploy to prevent him/her from tracking the flight of the incoming ball. In a more subtle vein, cricketers use verbal 'sledging' techniques to unsettle or distract their opponents. To illustrate, Shane Warne, one of the greatest bowlers in the history of the game, used to disrupt batsmen's concentration by getting them to think too much about their technique – which usually unravelled their skills (see discussion of paralysis by analysis in Chapter 4). Specifically, he admitted that,

> 'I'd try and get inside their head a bit, too. Sometimes, I'd just say to someone "You've changed your stance then?" – just to get them thinking, "Have I?"'[6]

Likewise, gamesmanship is well known in golf. For example, the late Seve Ballesteros earned a reputation as a tactical 'cougher'. On one occasion, Paul Azinger (USA) alleged that Ballesteros coughed strategically as a form of gamesmanship during the 1991 Ryder Cup match against Europe. In his defence Ballesteros claimed that he had suffered from a 'dust allergy' during the match in question! However, Ian Poulter subsequently complained about Ballesteros's coughing antics when he said:

> 'Initially, it came when I wasn't expecting it but I soon expected it all the time.'[7]

To make matters worse, when the coughing stopped, Ballesteros allegedly shuffled his feet while his opponent was putting!

Gamesmanship is also rife in tennis. For example, Maria Sharapova, a Wimbledon and US Open champion, was accused of 'legalised cheating' by a prominent coach (John Newcombe) because of her habit of grunting and screaming during rallies – a tactic that allegedly prevents opponents from hearing the ball coming off the strings of her racket and thereby predicting what type of shot they will face. Interestingly, Sharapova's screams have been recorded as being louder than the roar of a lion!

In snooker, extremely slow play has been associated with gamesmanship. For example, consider how slowly Peter Ebdon played when he defeated Ronnie O'Sullivan 13-11 in the quarter-finals of the 2005 World Snooker Championship in Sheffield. In the 20th frame of this match, Ebdon took 5 mins 30 secs to complete a break of 12 – which is 10 seconds *slower* than O'Sullivan had taken to complete a maximum 147 break at the same venue in 1997! Furthermore, Ebdon took 3 mins 5 secs for a single shot in the opening frame of final session. This slow play left O'Sullivan feeling so frustrated that he spent most of the time slumped in his chair – and even asked a spectator for the time at one stage during the second frame of the evening.

Internal distractions

Internal distractions include any thoughts, emotions (e.g., anger) and/or bodily sensations (e.g., pain, fatigue) that prevent you from concentrating fully on the job at hand. One such self-generated distraction comes from thinking too far ahead – wondering about what will happen in the future rather than focusing on what you have to do right now. Other internal distractions include worrying about what other people might say or do and focusing excessively on feelings of fatigue or anxiety.

Doug Sanders (Courtesy of Inpho Photography)

A classic example of a very costly internal distraction occurred in the case of the golfer Doug Sanders who missed a putt of less than three feet to win the 1970 British Open championship in St Andrews, Scotland. This error prevented him from winning his first major tournament and cost him millions of dollars in lost prize-money and endorsements. Remarkably, Sanders' mistake was triggered by thinking too far ahead – making a victory speech before the putt had been taken.

'I made the mistake about thinking which section of the crowd I was going to bow to! I had the victory speech prepared before the battle was over . . . I would give up every victory I had to have won that title. It's amazing how many different things to my normal routine I did on the 18th hole. There's something for psychologists there, the way that the final hole of a major championship can alter the way a man thinks.'[8]

As you can see from this quote, focusing on the wrong target caused Sanders to change his normal pre-putt routine.

Thinking too far ahead can also affect jockeys in horse-racing. To illustrate, Irish jumps jockey Roger Loughran learned a concentration lesson that he'll never forget when riding his horse, Central House, in the 'Dial-A-Bet' Chase at Leopardstown in 2005. Leading narrowly with about 90m to go, Loughran misperceived a stick on the finishing straight as the winning post and sat up in premature celebration – punching the air in front of a crowd of 20,000. Unfortunately, by the time he realised that he had made a mistake, Loughran had allowed two other riders to pass him. So, he ended up finishing third, not first, in the race and, to add insult to injury, was also banned for failing to ride through the finish. Rather unkindly, this lapse in concentration was described by the tabloid press as being a bad case of 'premature jockelation'(!) – and was estimated to have cost punters a large amount of money.

To summarise, in this section we've explained what distractions are, where they come from and how can impair your performance in sport. With these ideas in mind, let's explore the distractions that you experience.

Exploring your distractions

1. What things tend to upset your focus *before* a game/match? Give an example of the experience or situation and try to describe how it makes you feel and how it affects your performance. Was this distraction external or internal?
2. What distractions bother you *during* the event itself? Again, try to describe how it makes you feel and how it affects your performance. Was this distraction external or internal?
3. Looking back at these two experiences/situations, how would you like to have reacted to them? Remember – you can't change an external distraction but you *can* change how you react to it.

Now that we've explored your typical distractions, let's consider how you can develop more effective concentration skills.

Building good concentration

As we've indicated earlier, a good way to establish the building blocks of effective concentration is to explore the minds of athletes who have achieved peak performance in their sport. Research suggests that there are least five building blocks of effective concentration in sport.

1. You have to decide to concentrate – it won't just happen by chance

The first building block of effective concentration concerns 'conscious attention', which we introduced earlier in this chapter. The idea here is that you have to *decide* to invest mental effort in your performance. Put simply, you have to prepare to concentrate rather than simply hope that it will happen by chance. And in sport, there's a strong link between *deciding* to concentrate and subsequently performing to your full potential. For example, Tiger Woods revealed that before tournaments,

> *'I get into my own little world and my own little zone.'*[9]

A practical tip that might help you to get into your zone is to visualise a mental 'switch on' location before you enter your competitive environment. For example, you could imagine turning on your concentration switch when you change in the locker room before a match. This focusing technique was used by Martin Corry, the former England and Lions' rugby forward, who said that,

> *'I used to like switching the dressing room light off, to signify the end of our preparations and the start of something new.'*[10]

This idea of learning to switch on your concentration before you compete was nicely captured by Garry Sobers, one of the finest all-rounders in the history of cricket, when he proposed that,

> *'Concentration's like a shower. You don't turn it on until you want to bathe . . . You don't walk out of the shower and leave it running. You turn it off, you turn it on . . . It has to be fresh and ready when you need it.'*[11]

In summary, in order to focus properly you need to create an imaginary 'switch on' zone before you compete.

2. Be single-minded: Focus on one thought at a time

A second building block of effective concentration is the 'one thought' principle – the idea that you can focus consciously on only one thing at a time. This idea comes from the discovery that our working memory system (which controls our ability to pay attention) is very fragile and hence easily overloaded. So, to focus properly you need to be single-minded. For example, consider the views of Michael Phelps, the most decorated Olympian of all time with a total of 22 medals (including 18 golds) in swimming:

> 'You have to go one day at a time, one meet at a time, and one practice at a time.'[12]

3. Your mind is truly focused when you're doing what you're thinking

A third principle of good concentration is the idea that your mind is properly focused when there is no difference between what you are thinking about and what you are doing. For example, after Roger Bannister had run the first sub-four-minute mile run in May 1954 in Oxford, he revealed that,

> 'There was no pain, only a great unity of movement and aim.'[13]

We discovered this idea earlier in the chapter when we explained how Michael Johnson used to clear his mind to help him to focus on the jobs that he had to do. To ensure that, like Johnson, you *do* exactly what you are thinking, you must focus only on jobs that are under your control in any given sport situation.

4. Keep your mind on track: Re-focus when necessary

Fourth, as you are likely to encounter many distractions in your sport, you need to remind yourself to re-focus regularly so that your mind stays focused. One way of doing this is to write a personal symbol on your sports gear to remind you what to focus on. For example, after South African golfer Louis Oosthuizen had won the Open Championship at St Andrews in 2010, he said that he had used a red dot on his glove as a reminder to concentrate on the shot that he was playing.[14]

5. Focus outwards when you get nervous

The final building block of effective concentration is that if you get nervous, you must make sure to focus *outwards* on actions – and not inwards on doubts. Some athletes are so good at this skill that they play every shot as if it were the only one that mattered. For example, a story tells of the time that Jack Nicklaus, the famous golf champion, was one hole down with one to play in a match. Having hit a bad drive, he produced an amazing recovery shot to win the hole and draw the match. When asked afterwards how he had managed to concentrate under such pressure, he uttered the immortal words,

> 'The ball doesn't know the score!'[15]

Practical concentration techniques

Lots of techniques are available to help athletes to focus properly. The ones that we have found to work best are those that narrow the gap between what you're thinking and what you're doing. Let's explore each of these techniques now.

1. Set goals – focus on actions not results

The first practical tip on improving your concentration is to set performance or action goals for yourself every time you compete. These goals (e.g., 'keep up with play' or 'get your first serve in') are jobs that you can do no matter what the score is or who you're playing against. By focusing on actions that are under your control, you're less likely to be distracted than if you concentrate on the possible result of your match.

2. Use routines

A second concentration technique has already been outlined in Chapter 4 – use a consistent routine before you perform key skills. Routines take you from thinking about something to doing it. They are valuable because they help you to focus on the job you have to do, one step at a time. For example, if you are a tennis player, you may like to bounce the ball a certain number of times before you serve (maybe saying 'bounce', 'hit' at the same time to keep the right rhythm). Also, by concentrating on each step of your routine, you're encouraging yourself to stay in the present moment.

Developing a pre-shot routine in golf

Step 1: First, you have to *assess* the situation or 'check it out'. The task here is to gather all relevant information before planning your shot. In particular, you should pay attention to such key factors as the lie of the ball, the length of the grass, the direction and speed of any wind blowing, the distance between your ball and your target, and the existence of any special hazards.

Step 2: Having gathered this information, you must *plan* your shot. In this step, you have to decide on the type of shot you'd like to play, the most suitable club for that shot, and the best target for this shot. A useful tip here is to *stand behind the ball* while you grip the club and choose a specific target. The important thing is to be decisive, and once the decision is made, to draw a line. If you are still deciding when you are taking the shot, the outcome will be indecisive.

Step 3: The next step involves 'seeing' and 'feeling' the shot that you would like to play. Visualise this shot in your mind's eye as vividly as possible. For example, can you see the shape of the shot? Can you see it landing and bouncing close to your target? Once you've pictured it, get into the 'ready' position and align your club and body to the target. Then, take your preferred number of practice swings to establish the correct rhythm for the shot. As you rehearse your swing, feel the smooth *tempo* of the shot.

Step 4: The final step involves making yourself comfortable as you address the ball, clearing your mind of all thoughts, making any final adjustments to your stance, waggling your club, glancing at the target again, and then – letting your shot flow. This final stage of the routine is often quite difficult because it requires a lot of *trust* to move from thinking about your shot to actually playing it. To clear the mind of thought during the execution of the shot itself it may be helpful to say to yourself a word that characterises the action – flow, or swing are common examples.

Routines are the most popular concentration strategies used by top athletes. For example, Kelly Holmes spoke about the routine that helped her to achieve double-gold medal success for Britain at the 2004 Olympic Games in Athens:

'*After the first heat of the 800m, the races were always around the same time so I stuck to the same routine. I left for the track at the same time, I kept wearing my Team GB dog-tag around my neck, and it became my lucky charm, kissing it. When I went to the warm-up track, I would listen to Alicia Keyes singing 'If I ain't got you' and applied the words to the gold medal I wanted. I sang it as I warmed up and it brought tears to my eyes because I was dreaming of a gold medal. When I eventually got it, I kept the same routine for the 1500m. I cried before I left to run the 800m final because it was either going to be my dream or it would go all wrong and I cried again before the 1500m – I have been an emotional wreck.*'[16]

Routines can incorporate several proven concentration techniques. For example, the Irish rugby outside-half Ronan O'Gara combined imagery (see Chapter 6) and trigger words in his pre-kick routine before kicking the winning penalty in the 2006 final of the European Cup against Biarritz in Cardiff:

'*It was obvious how important it was, but I just had to get into my routine and block everything else out. Usually, there's a mark in the centre of the crossbar and I focus on that . . . I imagine a little hoop between the sticks, like a gymnasium hoop, and I picture the ball going through that. I stepped back and the buzz words in my mind were, "Stay tall and follow through."*'[17]

Kelly Holmes (Courtesy of Inpho Photography)

3. Use 'trigger words'

A third focusing technique involves the use of trigger words or short, vivid and positively phrased verbal reminders designed to help you focus on a specific target or to perform a relevant action. To illustrate, Paula Radcliffe, who has won both the London and New York marathons and who holds the current world record time for the women's marathon, uses a strategy which involves counting her steps silently to herself as a trigger to maintain her concentration in a race:

> 'When I count to 100 three times, it's a mile. It helps me to focus on the moment and not to think about how many miles I have to go. I concentrate on breathing and striding, and I go within myself.'[18]

4. Visualise what you want to do next

Another concentration strategy involves the use of mental imagery – 'seeing' and 'feeling' yourself performing a given skill in your mind's eye before you actually do it (see Chapter 6 for practical advice on using imagery). Imagery helps you to prepare for various imaginary scenarios, thereby ensuring that you will not be distracted by unexpected events. It can also help you to distinguish between 'on' and 'off' zones in competitive sport situations. For example, if you're a racket sports player, you could mark an imaginary 'performance zone' at the back of the court where you can switch on and off, as required.

Imagery is widely used in sport as a concentration technique. For example, rugby star Ronan O'Gara used imagery to focus on the execution of his last-minute drop-goal to help Ireland win the 2009 grand slam in the final match against Wales:

> '*I had the imagery and visualised the kick going over . . . I just had to get the ball up as opposed to drive it up.*'[19]

Similarly, the golfer Darren Clarke, who won the Open Championship in 2011, revealed how much he relies on mental imagery:

> '*Visualising things is massively important. If you don't visualise, then you allow other negative thoughts to enter your head. Not visualising is almost like having a satellite navigation system in your car, but not entering your destination into it. The machinery can only work if you put everything in there.*'[20]

5. Relax and centre your body

Physical relaxation techniques can help you to concentrate more effectively. For example, lowering your shoulders, doing gentle neck-rolling exercises, flapping out the tension from your arms and legs, and taking slow deep breaths can lower your centre of gravity and reduce the likelihood of error. Indeed, one of the biggest mistakes that novices in golf and tennis make is to hold in their breath while they prepare for a shot. If you do this, your muscles will tense up and your swing will be affected.

By contrast, exhaling while relaxing your muscles is widely used as a focusing technique in sport by stars such as former England and Lions rugby outside-half Jonny Wilkinson:

> '*As I got more into kicking, I became more involved in looking at other aspects, and one area I looked at was focusing from the inside, slowing down the breathing, relaxation, 'centering', which is a way of channelling my power and energy from my core, just behind my navel, down my left leg and into my left foot to get that explosive power.*'[21]

6. Simulation training: Try a dress rehearsal

Simulation training or dress rehearsal is based on the assumption that you can learn to concentrate more effectively in real-life pressure situations by training under conditions that recreate them in practice. For example, in 2008, England's Harlequins rugby team trained on their home ground at the Stoop under a giant screen playing loud music and YouTube clips in preparation for a noisy away match against Stade Français where 80,000 fans were expected to attend.[22] Harlequins won the match. Similarly, Bob Bowman, the renowned swimming coach, used adversity training to prepare Michael Phelps for his multiple gold-medal success at the 2008 Olympics. Specifically, he deliberately broke Phelps' goggles in training races so that he would be ready to cope if required to swim blindly in the Olympic finals. Remarkably, this very scenario occurred when Phelps was forced to swim without his goggles (after they filled with water) for the last 100m of the 200m butterfly event – which he duly won.[23]

A list of possible simulation techniques for counteracting distractions in soccer is provided in the table below.

Unfortunately, even the most ingenious simulations cannot fully replicate the arousal experienced by most athletes in actual competition. For example, if you're a rugby place kicker, a good way of replicating match conditions in training is to run up and down for a few minutes before taking penalties. After that, you should stop, lower your arousal levels and follow your pre-kick routine. The purpose of this short bout of high intensity exercise is to increase your heart-rate sufficiently to simulate what it would be like to have to take a kick during actual match conditions.

The last word

In this chapter, we explained that 'concentration', or the ability to focus on what is most important in any situation while ignoring distractions, is vital for athletic success. It's like a mental spotlight that you shine at things (either in the world around you or inside your own head) that interest you. Unfortunately, you'll find it difficult to stay focused for long in competitive sport because of the number and variety of distractions that you encounter there. The good news, however, is that concentration is a mental skill that you can improve with knowledge and

Simulation training in soccer: Practical suggestions

Distraction	*Possible simulation technique*
Crowd noise	Playing pre-recorded CDs of crowd noise during training sessions in order to familiarise players with expected distractions during away matches
Gamesmanship	Arranging for team-mates to simulate opponents' gamesmanship during training sessions or practice matches
Fatigue	Alternating normal training sessions with short bouts of high-intensity exercise to induce tiredness
Heat/humidity	Arranging for players to train and play while wearing layers of extra clothing to simulate hot weather effects
Unfavourable refereeing decisions	Designing 'modified' games containing deliberately biased umpiring decisions
Pressure	Simulating pressure situations in training (e.g., practising with your team losing 1-0 with 5 minutes to go)

practice. To boost your knowledge, we explained what distractions are, where they come from and the five key building blocks of effective concentration (e.g., you have to decide to concentrate – it won't just happen by chance). Turning from theory to practice, we showed you six simple but powerful focusing techniques that you can use in your sport to keep your mind on the right track (e.g., routines, trigger words, mental practice). Putting it all together, we'll leave the last word on concentration to diver Tom Daley, a world champion in 2009 and a medallist at the 2012 Olympic Games:

'I go into my own little bubble and . . . the results look after themselves.'[24]

6   Using your imagination

Have you ever imagined yourself in your 'mind's eye' hitting a great golf shot or making a perfect pass to a team-mate before actually playing it? If so, you're in good company because many world-class athletes use their imagination to rehearse exactly what they want to do next in sport situations. For example, just before he scored a last-minute drop goal against Wales to help Ireland win the 2009 Six Nations rugby championship, Ronan O'Gara revealed that,

> 'I picked out three numbers in the stand behind the posts. I can still picture them perfectly. That was my target. I visualised the ball going through and kept that image. I played it in my mind a few times . . . this is what it comes down to now. One chance.'[1]

By combining such insights from sports stars with the latest research findings in psychology, we'll explain in this chapter why your ability to 'see' and 'feel' a skill before you perform is vital for success in sport. Put simply, we'll show you how to use your mind's eye to give your sporting skills a winning edge.

The pros and cons of using imagery: What you 'see' is (nearly always) what you get

Athletes, coaches and psychologists have known for a long time that mental imagery, or your ability to 'see', 'hear' and 'feel' information in your mind that is not currently being perceived by your senses, is a powerful tool. If it is used systematically and positively, it can boost your skills and performance. For example, Jenson Button, the Formula One star who won the 2009 World Drivers' Championship, regularly rehearses his gear shifts in his imagination before a race:

> 'I'll sit down on a Swiss ball with a steering wheel in my hands and close my eyes. I'll drive around the circuit, practising every gear shift. It's just a little bit of visualisation work . . .'[2]

Likewise, your imagination can also enhance your psychological skills. For example, the famous athlete Roger Bannister used imagery to calm his nerves before he ran the world's first sub-four-minute mile in 1954:

Roger Bannister breaking four-minute mile (Courtesy of Inpho Photography)

'Each night in the week before the race, there came a moment when I saw myself at the starting line. My whole body would grow nervous and tremble. I ran the race over in my mind. Then I would calm myself and sometimes get off to sleep.'[3]

In recent years, imagery techniques have become extremely popular in sport psychology for four main reasons. First, imagery is spontaneous and effortless in everyday life (e.g., we engage in it when packing the boot of a car or moving furniture from one room to another). Second, you can use imagery anywhere (e.g., on the practice field, in the locker-room) and at any time – even when you're physically injured. Third, as we've illustrated, imagery is a versatile tool which can be used to improve mental (e.g., the ability to relax, focus) as well as technical skills (e.g., the putting stroke in golf – see later in the present chapter). Finally, imagery guidelines are well grounded in a wealth of psychological theory and research.[4]

So far, so good – imagery definitely works. But to make it work *effectively*, you need to avoid three common mistakes. First, you have to be very careful about *exactly what* you imagine. For example, consider what can happen in a sport like darts, archery or golf when you visualise the wrong target – something that you're trying to avoid rather than hit. This use of negative imagery is most likely to happen when you're nervous. To illustrate, let's imagine that you're a golfer standing on the tee-box of a tricky dog-leg hole. Having identified a target to aim your drive at, you suddenly notice a large water hazard to the right of the fairway. Because you're worried that your ball might end up in the water, you think to yourself, 'I hope I don't hit that lake'. Sadly, that's exactly what happens a moment later as you slice your drive and watch helplessly as it plops into the water. In this case, you've made the classic mistake of engaging in negative imagery before you perform a skill – 'seeing' a target that you want to *avoid* (the ball hitting the lake) rather than one that you want to hit (reaching a specific spot on the fairway). More generally, this example shows us that your mind does not distinguish clearly between positive and negative targets. So, in golf, as in other target sports, the last image that you have in your mind before you strike the ball is the one that will guide your aim. The lesson is clear: You must imagine a *positive* target in order to improve your performance in sport.

A second caution about imagery is that you shouldn't confuse deliberate mental rehearsal with aimless daydreaming. Although both of these processes use imagery, the difference is that whereas daydreams are usually *fantasy-based* (e.g., imagining holding the World Cup trophy aloft as the captain of your national team), deliberate mental rehearsal is *action-focused* – 'seeing' and 'feeling' yourself performing a specific sport skill in vivid detail. To illustrate this latter idea, consider how swimmer Michael Phelps, the most decorated Olympian of all time, used imagery to prepare for competition:

> '*I can visualise how I want the perfect race to go. I can see the start, the strokes, the walls, the turns, the finish, the strategy, all of it.*'[5]

A third problem with imagery is that people often use it to *replay the past* rather than to rehearse or anticipate an action in the future. Unfortunately, going over a silly mistake or a missed opportunity in your mind's eye after a match is not only frustrating but also rather pointless unless you can use this experience to correct some flaws in your game. In general, imagery is more likely to be effective when it's used in *preview* rather than *review* mode.

Despite these problems afflicting certain types of imagery, visualisation is a popular and effective performance-enhancement technique in sport. However, before we show you how to use it to your advantage, let's try to explain what happens in our mind's eye when we imagine something.

Inside the mind's eye: What really happens in your brain's magic theatre

Although we often take mental imagery for granted, we should really pause to marvel at this astonishing skill because it allows us to create virtual experiences of the world – to simulate things (e.g., sensations, movements, people, places and situations) that aren't immediately evident to our senses. To illustrate, when you close your eyes and imagine yourself kicking a ball, you experience sensations that seem real even though you're not actually moving your limbs. Based on such experiences, imagery is often portrayed as a kind of private film theatre where you can look at mental pictures with your mind's eye whenever you wish.

Interestingly, this magic theatre analogy is often evoked in sport when athletes describe their imagery experiences. For example, Jack Nicklaus, arguably the most successful golfer of all time, famously revealed that he always used to imagine a shot before he hit it:

> '*I never hit a shot, even in practice, without having a sharp, in-focus picture of it in my head.*'[6]

Similarly, Luke Donald, who was ranked as the world's best golfer in 2011, claimed that he relies on imagery to such an extent that he thinks in pictures not words:

> '*I can't explain how I'm going to hit a shot 230 yards straight (but) . . . I can picture it in my mind.*'[7]

Intriguingly, some athletes go to extraordinary lengths to make their mental images as vivid as possible. For example, the famous Swiss double-Olympic bobsled champion Gustav Weder was allegedly so meticulous in his imagery homework that he took photographs of the Winter Olympic course and mentally rehearsed on it every day before the competition began.[8]

Nicklaus and Donald emphasise the visual aspects of imagery. But do we really look at pictures in our mind when we imagine something? Although it's superficially plausible, the 'pictures in the mind' metaphor of imagery is quite misleading because many of our images are actually *non-visual* in nature. For example, if you close your eyes, you should be able to imagine the sound of a crowd cheering (an auditory image), the texture of a golf-ball (a tactile image), the 'taste' of chlorine in the swimming pool (a gustatory image), the smell of 'wintergreen' in the changing room (an olfactory image), or the feeling of tightness in your muscles that occurs when you cycle up a steep hill (a kinaesthetic image). Clearly, most of our everyday imaginary experiences are multi-sensory in nature. To illustrate, you can easily combine visual and auditory images when you 'see' yourself taking a penalty kick in soccer and then 'hear' the ball hitting the net. This example leads us to an intriguing question. What happens in our brain's 'magic theatre' when we imagine performing an action?

In order to answer this question, we need a strong scientific theory (about what psychological processes underlie mental imagery) and a precise method (to identify which parts of the brain 'light up' when people rehearse actions in their imagination). Theoretically, imagery involves perception without sensation – running perception backwards.[9] To explain, whereas perception occurs whenever we interpret sensory input, imagery arises when we interpret memorised information. For example, you need to have a muscular memory of what taking a penalty kick involves before you can rehearse it in your imagination. Methodologically, neuroimaging (brain scanning) techniques reveal that similar parts of the brain 'light up' when we *imagine* things as when we perceive them or even think about doing them. More precisely, the occipital cortex or visual centre of the brain (which is located at the back of the head) is triggered when people

Bobsleigh (Courtesy of iStockphoto)

are asked to visualise things.[10] Similarly, when dancers use motor imagery to imagine performing certain skills, the parts of the brain that become active are those that are involved in planning and executing the actual movements involved.[11] In short, perception, imagery and motor control share some common brain regions.

Now that we've explained what happens in your mind's eye during imagery, let's consider some of the key characteristics of mental images.

Images differ in vividness . . .

To begin with, mental images differ from each other in their vividness, clarity or realism. A 'vivid' image is one that clearly resembles the experience that it simulates. Typically, the greater the number of senses that you use to create an image, the more vivid the resulting experience. A simple way of developing your imagery vividness skills is to practise paying attention to an object from your sport (e.g., a tennis racket or a golf ball) using all your senses. Focus particularly on what it looks like (e.g., what colour is it, does it have a logo?), what it feels like (is it rough or smooth?), how heavy it is, and whether or not it has a distinctive smell.

Images differ in controllability . . .

A second way in which images differ from each other is in their controllability or the ease with which you can manipulate them for a specific purpose. Here's a test of your controllability skills.

The tennis ball test

Can you imagine holding a bright yellow tennis ball in your right hand and then throwing it into the air? Can you see its arc as it stops and begins to fall back down? Can you imagine catching this ball and then bouncing it three times on the wooden floor of your room? If you found these images easy to create, you probably have good control over your mental imagery.

And images differ in the feelings and emotions they evoke . . .

A third feature of mental images is that they tend to evoke feelings (e.g., imagine how hard it would be to lift a heavy filing cabinet) and emotions (recall how Roger Bannister trembled with anticipation when he imagined himself competing in an important race). Can you visualise yourself as a novice rock-climber standing on the ledge of a cliff face, not knowing what to do next? This image should make you feel a little queasy. By contrast, can you imagine yourself scoring the winning goal for your country in the World Cup final? Hopefully, this time, you should feel a surge of pleasant excitement.

To summarise, we've made three key points about imagery in this section. First, neuroimaging research shows when the brain forms a mental image of a skill, it uses a great deal of the neural circuitry that is involved in actually executing the action in question. Second, mental images are multi-sensory experiences that enable us to bring to mind sensations of absent people, objects, events and/or skills. Finally, images vary in vividness, controllability and in the feelings and emotions that they evoke.

Using imagery: Practical tips

Practise!

Remember that mental imagery is a skill that must be practised regularly for mastery – just like any other skill. For example, if you are a basketball player practising free throws, try to close your eyes for a second to 'see' and 'feel' each shot before you play it.

Be positive

When using your imagination, develop the habit of visualising a positive target (something to aim at) rather than a negative one (something that you want to avoid). For example, if you are a canoeist, try to picture your line through the gate. Remember, what you see is what you'll get.

Visualise specific actions rather than general results

In order to avoid daydreaming, it is better to visualise actions rather than results or scores. For example, in bowls, try to picture the shot that you want to play next rather than the score that you'd like to have for that end.

Use all relevant senses when forming your image

To increase the vividness of your images, try to combine as many as possible of the senses as are relevant to the skill that you'd like to practise. For example, if you're mentally rehearsing a penalty kick in rugby, you should be able to 'feel' the turf under your feet and the weight of the ball as you place it on the ground. You should also be able to 'hear' the sound of the ball as you strike it and to 'see' its flight as you curl it between the posts.

Use imagery in practice sessions

Visualisation works best when it is alternated with periods of physical practice. So, you should develop the habit of spending a moment or two mentally rehearsing a skill or movement just before you go to start a training session.

Getting things in perspective

So far, we've introduced mental imagery, outlined what happens in your brain when you imagine something and sketched some properties of images. However, not everyone imagines things in exactly the same way. For instance, when you kick a ball in your mind's eye, do you see yourself on a screen as if you're watching *someone else* performing the skill or do you feel as though *you're* actually kicking the ball? There is an interesting difference between these two visual perspectives, as we'll now explain.

Briefly, when you create a visual mental image of a skill, you have a choice of two perspectives to adopt. On the one hand, you could visualise yourself performing this skill as if you were watching a video replay on a screen. This approach is called 'external' visual imagery because it involves viewing your actions from outside your body. On the other hand, you could combine various sensory experiences to create a feeling of what it would be like to perform the skill yourself – rather than watching someone else do it. In this case, you are using 'internal' or within-body imagery. Let's clarify this distinction using a golfing example. If you were visualising yourself playing golf on a wet and windy day from an *internal* perspective, you should be able to picture yourself hitting the ball and also to feel the weight of the club in your hands and the wind and rain on your face. In this case, the multi-sensory nature of your imagery experience increases its vividness. If you find it difficult to imagine a skill from an internal perspective, it may help to pay attention to the feelings that are generated in each of your senses as you practise this skill.

Are you an internal or external? The clock face test

Many of us tend to have a dominant imagery style, either internal or external. As a 'cheap and cheerful' way to explore which could be your dominant style, ask someone to help with this simple exercise.

With their forefinger, ask the person to draw the two hands of a clock on your forehead, with the clock's hands pointing to either 3 o'clock or 9 o'clock – but they mustn't tell you what they drew.

Instantaneously you should say what you think they drew.

If you are correct, then your dominant style may well be external (that is, you are looking from the outside in) but if your dominant style is internal then it is more likely that you get it wrong (you are looking from the inside out and so are more likely to report the mirror image).

Having explained and examined this distinction between external and internal imagery perspectives theoretically, let's now consider a sporting example, adapted from an exercise devised by Tony Morris, Michael Spittle and Anthony Watt.[12]

Imagery at the pool

In order to explore two different ways of looking at things in your mind's eye, let's imagine that you are a swimmer about to compete in a 100m freestyle race.

External imagery

'Imagine standing on the blocks along with the other competitors who are lined up on either side of you. You can see yourself as if you were on a large video screen, looking confident and relaxed. Although the other swimmers are standing to your left and right, your eyes are focused on the water in the pool, which looks blue and inviting. You adjust your cap and goggles and prepare for the starter's command. When you hear "On your marks!", you bend forward – poised and ready for a powerful start. At the sound of the beep, you take off and dive like an arrow into the pool. You are completely immersed in the water and hear nothing. All you can see is your streamlined shape under the water. You break the surface, kick hard and glide through the pool using strong and powerful strokes. You're aware that the other swimmers are beginning to fall behind as you surge towards the wall. As you reach it, you start the turn. Flipping over, you can see yourself pushing hard against the wall as your body is submerged. The shape of your streamlined body is visible under the surface. As your head breaks the surface again, you can see that you're still in the lead. Looking totally focused, you glide through the water using powerful strokes.'

Internal imagery

'Imagine standing on the blocks along with the other competitors who are lined up on either side of you. You feel that you are really there. You look around at the other competitors and are fully aware of all the sights and sounds around the pool. You can smell the chlorine at the pool and the water seems inviting. You adjust your cap and goggles until they feel just right and bounce up and down on your toes as you wait for the starter's command. When you hear "On your marks!", you bend forward slowly and prepare your body for a powerful start. At the sound of the beep, you take off and dive like an arrow into the pool. As soon as you hit the water, your body feels completely immersed. Your body feels streamlined and you kick hard. When you break the surface, you kick hard again and you can feel your powerful strokes helping you to glide through the pool. You're aware that the other swimmers are beginning to fall behind as you surge towards the wall. As you reach it, you start the turn. Flipping over, you can feel yourself pushing hard against the wall as your body is submerged. You start the turn,

> throwing your legs over your head and pushing your streamlined body tight and hard. As your head breaks the surface, you can see that you're still in the lead. Feeling totally focused, you glide through the water using powerful strokes' (based on Morris et al., 2005).

Which imagery perspective is better?

An obvious question that arises from this exercise is which of the two imagery perspectives is better? There is no clear answer to this question for two main reasons.

First, most athletes tend to switch their perspective as they become more proficient in their chosen sport. Indeed, research shows that about 25 per cent of expert canoeists can 'feel' the muscular movements involved in paddling – even when they're viewing themselves from an external visual imagery perspective.[13]

Second, each perspective has its own strengths and weaknesses. Specifically, the benefit of an external perspective is that it allows you to inspect your actions from different positions, thereby enabling you to 'zoom in' on any problematic aspects of your technique. By contrast, the benefit of using an internal imagery perspective is that it should enhance the vividness or realism of the imaginary action. Not surprisingly, different sport skills may benefit from mental rehearsal using different imagery perspectives. For example, external imagery may be helpful for skills such as gymnastics or rock-climbing where body 'form' or shape is important. On the other hand, internal imagery may be more suitable for skills that depend on perceptual sequencing such as slalom skiing or self-paced skills such as the free-throw in basketball.

Now that we've outlined the main differences between external and internal imagery perspectives, let's summarise some key research findings on imagery use in sport.

What we know about imagery use in sport

Based on hundreds of studies of imagery in sport, a number of conclusions have emerged as follows.

1. Visual and kinaesthetic imagery are most common among athletes

Among the most popular forms of imagery used by athletes are visual and kinaesthetic (feeling-oriented) imagery. Sometimes, these two types of imagery are combined. For example, Tiger Woods claimed that,

> 'You have to see the shots and feel them through your hands.'[14]

2. Imagery is used more frequently by elite athletes than by less skilled ones

Research shows that highly-skilled athletes tend to use imagery more often than do less skilled athletes.[15]

3. Imagery is especially common before competition

Athletes tend to use imagery more in pre-competitive than in training situations.[16] This finding suggests that athletes use their imagination more for performance-enhancement in competition than for skill-improvement in practice.

4. Imagery can be motivational as well as skill-focused

Athletes appear to use imagery for motivational as well as for cognitive purposes.[17] For example, if you find it difficult to motivate yourself to go for a run on a cold and windy winter's night, try imagining how satisfied you'll feel when you have a hot shower after you come home from your exercise. Clearly, imagery can help you to visualise *rewards* as well as goals.

5. Imagery isn't always used positively

Despite the well-known benefits of using positive imagery, many sports performers reported experiencing negative images involving the anticipation of mistakes, setbacks and bad results.[18]

Applications of imagery in sport

If you're an athlete, you can use imagery for a variety of purposes, including skill learning and practice (e.g., mentally rehearsing skills such as goal kicking or free-throwing), developing tactical strategies (e.g., formulating a game plan in your mind for a forthcoming match), preparation for competition (e.g., using imagery to familiarise yourself with a match venue), improving psychological skills (e.g., using imagery to reduce your anxiety, increase your confidence and improve your concentration) and injury rehabilitation (e.g., closing your eyes and feeling the stretch in the back of your leg as you engage in physiotherapy exercise for a torn calf muscle). Let's now give you some examples of these imagery applications.

1. Mental practice

Earlier, we used some examples to show you that you can use imagery to 'see' and 'feel' yourself performing key sport skills in your imagination before actually doing them. As this is probably the most common application of imagery in sport, we'll give you some practical tips on effective mental practice in the next section.

2. Developing tactical strategies

You can also use imagery for strategic reasons, such as formulating a game plan before a competitive event. For example, David Hemery, an Olympic champion for Britain in the 400m hurdles race in the 1968 Games, revealed the role of imagination in his success:

> 'Before the race, I tried to visualise every eventuality, every lane draw, every kind of weather condition and running one-to-one against the competitors . . .'[19]

3. Dress-rehearsal for competition

You can use imagery as a form of 'dress rehearsal' for a competitive situation. For example, consider how Wayne Rooney visualises himself playing as well as possible before a match:

> 'I lie in bed the night before the game and visualize myself scoring goals or doing well. You're trying to put yourself in that moment and trying to prepare yourself, to have a "memory" before the game.'[20]

4. Reducing anxiety

Imagery can also help you to feel relaxed and to behave calmly in anticipated stressful situations. Richard Faulds (the British shooter) created the image of an 'ice-man' prior to winning the 2000 Olympic gold medal for trap-shooting:

> 'The image is the ice-man. You walk like an ice-man and think like an ice-man.'[21]

Wayne Rooney (Courtesy of Inpho Photography)

5. Increasing confidence

Many athletes report that a relationship exists between imagery and confidence. This link is captured insightfully by Nick Faldo, a six-time major champion golfer. Speaking of the time in the early 1990s when he won three major tournaments, he said,

> 'In each of those weeks, I had total confidence in what I was doing. I was picking a shot, visualising it and trusting myself to pull it off. I could stand up there and do precisely what I intended to do.'[22]

6. Improving concentration

As we explained in Chapter 5, mental imagery is used widely by athletes as a concentration strategy. For example, the football star Ronaldinho, a World Cup winner with Brazil, stated that,

> 'When I train, one of the things I concentrate on is creating a mental picture of how best to deliver that ball to a team-mate, preferably leaving him alone in front of the rival goalkeeper.'[23]

7. Recovering from injury

You can also use imagery to assist physical rehabilitation from injury. When Steve Backley (the British javelin thrower who won medals at three successive Olympic Games between 1992 and 2000) was unable to walk or train after he had sprained an ankle some years ago, he began to use imagery as part of his rehabilitation. Sitting in a chair, he imagined himself throwing the javelin in each of the world's top sports stadia. Astonishingly, he estimated afterwards that he had mentally 'hurled' over 1,000 javelins during that period of injury.[24] Even more remarkably, when he returned to competition a few weeks later, he continued where he had left off before the injury and achieved his Olympic goals.

Mental practice: Five practical tips

As we explained earlier in this chapter, mental practice (MP) involves systematically rehearsing skills in your mind's eye before actually performing them. Although it may seem like a modern discovery, MP is not a new technique at all. In fact, scientific interest in mental practice is as old as the discipline of psychology itself. Over a century ago, William James suggested, rather counter-intuitively, that you actually learn to skate in the summer and to swim in the winter – because of the way in which you anticipate experiences using your imagination.[25] Since that era, the effects of mental practice on skilled performance have been reviewed extensively by psychologists.[26] From such reviews, a number of conclusions have emerged as follows.

Steve Backley (Courtesy of Inpho Photography)

1. MP can improve your skills

Compared to not practising at all, MP improves skilled performance. Of course, MP is less effective than physical practice in helping people to master sport skills – presumably because it doesn't provide any actual muscular feedback to the practitioner.

2. MP works best when it's combined with physical practice

When combined and alternated with physical practice, MP tends to produce better skill learning than that which results from either mental or physical practice alone.

3. MP is especially helpful for cognitive skills

Although mental practice is especially suitable for rehearsing cognitive sport skills (i.e., those that involve some degree of sequential planning such as skiing, paddling, motor sports or equestrian events), it can also help to increase strength performance (e.g., in weightlifting).

4. MP is more suitable for elite than for novice athletes

In general, mental practice tends to be more effective for those who are already proficient in the skills that they are trying to improve. Novices do not benefit

from MP as much as experts because their mental 'blueprint' of the skill in question is not very well established.

5. MP is more effective for people with good imagery skills

Available evidence suggests that those who are adept at generating and controlling vivid images tend to benefit more from mental practice than do people who lack such imagery abilities.

In summary, there is now abundant evidence that mental practice is a powerful and effective technique for improving the learning and performance of a variety of sport skills. These skills include not only 'closed' (or self-paced) actions such as golf putting, tennis serving or penalty-taking but also 'open' (or reactive) ones such as volleying in tennis or tackling in soccer or rugby. But how exactly does mental practice work?

Although many theories of MP have been proposed since the 1930s, the psychological mechanisms that underlie it are still unclear. Nevertheless, of these theories, the most popular are the 'neuromuscular' model, the cognitive account, 'bio-informational' theory and the PETTLEP approach.[27] Briefly, the neuro-muscular model proposes that imagining an action causes faint activity in the muscles that are used to perform the skill in question. This faint activity helps you to practise the skill as if you were actually doing it. By contrast, cognitive theories claim that MP helps you to pay attention to and remember key elements of the skill being rehearsed. In other words, it works by changing your mental 'blueprint' of the skill or movement that you're trying to master. Third, the 'bio-informational' theory claims that MP effects reflect a complex interaction between three factors – the environment in which the movement in question is performed ('stimulus' information), what is felt as the movement occurs ('response' information) and the perceived importance of this skill to the performer ('meaning' information). Finally, the PETTLEP model[28] proposes that mental practice works best when it replicate athletes' competitive environment as well as the emotions that they experience when performing.

At this stage, however, let's leave the theories aside and take you through a mental practice exercise in golf putting.

Golf putting . . . in your mind's eye

The purpose of this exercise is to help you to 'see' and 'feel' your putting stroke in your mind's eye. By learning to visualise this stroke, you can practise it even when you're not playing golf. Please make sure that you are sitting comfortably with your eyes closed and that you will not be disturbed for the next few minutes.

Imagine standing on the green of a particular hole at your local golf course on a bright summer morning. The flag is lying to the side of the green casting a small shadow from the sun and you are all alone. Your ball is lying about a metre from the hole and you are standing comfortably beside it. As you look at the ball, you can see it glistening in the sunshine and feel the weight of your putter in your hand. You can also feel the springy grass underneath your feet.

Walking slowly to one side, you stand behind the ball and crouch down to assess the situation – noting a slight slope to the left. After a few seconds, you begin to see the best line for your putt and to make absolutely sure, you imagine drawing a white line between the hole and your ball. Slowly, you allow your eyes to gaze back and forth along this white line – back and forth, back and forth. Your target for this line is a slightly yellowish blade of grass which lies about a foot from where your ball lies. You look at this blade of grass to remind you of the line you have chosen.

Then you stand up slowly and approach the ball. Standing directly over the ball, you lower your shoulders, get comfortable and adjust your feet so that you're standing square to your putting line. Your set-up feels nice and relaxed and you breathe out gently – slowly and deliberately. Then, keeping your head still, you take two or three gentle practice swings – feeling your shoulders, arms and putter working together as a solid unit. Feel the smooth follow-through of your practice swing each time. Now, you're ready. So, you glance at the hole one more time, focus on the yellow blade of grass, and then release your swing. Slowly and gently, you guide the ball down the line.

Having examined the theory of MP and given you an example of how it works in golf, let's now turn to the practical question of how you can apply this technique to your own sports.

Mental practice (MP): Four steps to success

Mental practice or MP involves four steps. First, you have to prepare your mind by relaxing as much as possible. Second, you have to create the mental image of the skill which you wish to practise. Third, you should try to recall a successful performance of that skill by 'replaying' it in your mind. Finally, you should programme this imagery rehearsal into your mental preparation by combining it with a pre-performance routine.

Before you begin these steps, however, you must be quite clear and specific about the specific skill or situation that you'd like to rehearse in your mind's eye. So, let's start by pausing for a moment to pick a specific skill that you would like to practise in your mind.

Mental practice (MP) in action

The skill which I want to practise is _____

When did you last perform this skill correctly? _____

(We ask this question so that you will bring to mind a specific example of yourself performing this skill successfully.)

Now that we've picked a skill to work on, let's explore the four steps of mental practice.

Step 1: Relax

People visualise best when they are relaxed. That's one of the reasons why you often find yourself daydreaming as you sit comfortably in a bus or train. In general, imagery occurs spontaneously in our minds when we feel relaxed. One of the best ways to relax your body is through a deep breathing exercise – with your *diaphragm* rather than your chest. Before you begin this exercise, sit down in a quiet place and close your eyes. Now, slowly 'centre' your body by lowering your shoulders gently. Then, gently flap out any tension in your arms and legs. After that, take ten deep breaths, making sure that you're pushing your stomach *out* slowly when you breathe in and pulling *in* your stomach gently when you breathe out. Over time, you can train your body to relax even better by saying the word 'RELAX' to yourself as you breathe deeply. One way of doing this is to say **'RE'** when you breathe **in** – and **'LAX'** as you breathe **out**.

Step 2: Create your image

Now that you feel relaxed, you will find it easier to create the situation or skill that you wish to visualise. Think of and picture a skill or movement that you wish to improve in your next training/practice session. Close your eyes and imagine the venue where you will be performing this skill. Now try to see yourself doing this skill. Take a few minutes to imagine this scene as vividly as possible – notice details of the sights, sounds and bodily sensations which you are experiencing.

Step 3: Rehearse

Now see and feel yourself performing the skill slowly, smoothly and correctly. Notice how calm and confident you feel as you perform the movements in your mind. At first, it may help to slow down the movements – as though you're watching a slow-motion video of yourself playing the skill perfectly.

As you get better at visualisation, however, you should form images in 'real time' (i.e., at same speed as in real life). Watch yourself performing this skill over and over again for a moment or two.

Step 4: Make routine

Combining visualisation with a pre-performance routine is a technique for improving your concentration. As we explained in Chapter 4, a pre-performance routine is simply a series of actions that prepares you for your stroke/skill. It is like the steps of a staircase that takes you to your favourite place – your quiet zone where you will be free from distractions. At the beginning and end of your routine, visualise clearly what you want to achieve in your performance.

The last word

A key theme of this book is that although sport is played with the body, it's won in the mind. This idea is especially relevant to mental imagery or 'seeing' and 'feeling' a skill in your imagination before you actually perform it. We began this chapter by explaining that what you 'see' in your mind's eye – whether it's something that you want to do next or something that you hope to avoid – is nearly always what you get. So, the first point to remember is that for best results, what you imagine in sport should always be positive and action-focused. Having explored what happens in your brain when you imagine something, we showed you how to create mental images from two different perspectives – external (e.g., seeing yourself performing the skill as if you were watching yourself doing it on a television screen) and internal (feeling yourself performing the action as if you were *actually* doing it). Our third lesson is that you can use imagery for a wide range of different purposes in sport. Finally, going from theory to practice, we showed you how to use mental imagery to rehearse a sport skill in your mind's eye before you execute it.

7 Handling setbacks and mistakes

Although it's difficult to accept defeat or failure in any aspect of life, it's surprisingly easy to develop the habit of regarding such setbacks as someone else's fault. This tendency to blame other people for our own misfortunes is widespread in sport. For example, in soccer, after England's disappointing performance at the 2010 World Cup in South Africa, the players blamed their manager at the time, Fabio Capello. They claimed that he had picked the wrong team, played the wrong formation and had erred in his substitutions![1] Such a barrage of blame led Gareth Southgate (a former England international player) to observe that,

'We are breeding players that look for excuses, that don't want to take responsibility.'[2]

Psychologically, evading responsibility rather than looking in the mirror (see Chapter 3) is ultimately self-defeating. The problem is that if you play the 'blame game' regularly as a performer, *you're the one* who will lose out in the end because you will have denied yourself something very valuable – the possibility of *learning* from the feedback (however unpleasant) that any setback provides.

Based on the idea that we can learn a lot from adversity, the purpose of this chapter is twofold. First, we'll show you how to develop a helpful way of 'framing', or looking constructively at, setbacks in sport so that you can either learn from them or use them to motivate you in some way. Second, we'll equip you with some practical advice on developing effective mistake-management techniques.

At the outset, let's clarify an important point. Mistakes aren't always bad for us in sport, especially if we can use them to our advantage. An example of this latter possibility comes from the world of snooker. Briefly, in the 1997 Thailand Open, Nigel Bond staged a remarkable comeback to defeat the world champion at that time, Stephen Hendry. The most surprising aspect of this comeback, however, was that it was triggered by an error! To explain, because Bond had thought that the match was a best of *11* rather than 9 frames, he was not unduly perturbed by Hendry's early lead in the game and played in a relaxed frame of mind, not realising how close he was to defeat.

Strictly speaking, it wasn't really a mistake that boosted Bond's performance. It was actually his ability to stay calm when he fell behind that made all the difference. More generally, mistakes can provide helpful feedback to us because they define the limits of our performance at any given time. This idea that mistakes mark boundaries has an important practical implication for the way in which we practise. In particular, if you receive positive feedback on almost everything you do in sport, you won't improve your skills very much because you'll be working too close to your comfort zone. So, in order to avoid 'coasting' on talent alone, you have to be adventurous – and willing to challenge yourself by extending the boundaries of your performance. This point was captured clearly by the golfer Pádraig Harrington, a three-time major winner, when he said,

> 'You can't be great at anything unless you explore it right to the edge and if you're going to the edge, mistakes will definitely follow. That's the way it is. If you're looking for the comfort of not making mistakes and not failing, you'll finish up mediocre . . . But reaching greatness requires falling off the edge a load of times and having the courage to get back up and get on with it.'[3]

Harrington's quotation leads us to the main theme of this chapter – the idea that to achieve success in sport you must be able to put your mistakes and setbacks behind you and simply 'get on with it'. Such mental toughness in action is illustrated by the resilience of Jonny Wilkinson and Rory McIlroy. To explain, Wilkinson missed *three* drop-goals before scoring the one that helped England to a 20-17 extra-time victory over Australia in the 2003 World Cup rugby final. The learning point here is that despite three failed goal attempts, Wilkinson persisted – and eventually succeeded. Similarly, Rory McIlroy, a two-time golf major champion and top player in the world in 2012, used the setback of choking spectacularly under pressure on the last day of the 2011 US Masters as a spur to motivate him for the US Open tournament which he won just eight weeks later:

> 'Part of the motivation I had (at the US Open) was trying to prove something to myself, that I wasn't one of these players who crumbles under pressure, who folds, or chokes . . . I wanted to show them that the person they saw on that Sunday in Augusta was not the real Rory McIlroy.'[4]

Getting on with it

Psychologically, the ability to bounce back from adversity requires three important steps.

First, you need to develop the *right attitude* to setbacks from the beginning. Typically, winners in sport tend to 'frame' their errors as temporary misfortunes that are caused by factors that can be changed in the future – not irreversible catastrophes! Put simply, mistakes challenge us to work harder on our skills. Unfortunately, most of us fail to grasp this challenge because we tend to seek excuses for making errors.

Second, you need to *check your assumptions* from time to time. This step involves looking in the mirror (see Chapter 3) and addressing some deep-seated beliefs about your sporting performance. For example, do you *really* expect to play flawlessly all the time? If so, then your impossible standards are setting you up for a hard fall. Remember that in competitive sport, your performance is always a compromise between what you'd ideally like to achieve and what is possible in the prevailing circumstances. To illustrate, let's imagine that you're a good tennis player who loves to play an attacking serve-and-volley style in every match. That's a noble aspiration but is clearly unrealistic on certain occasions. For example, you'll have to make compromises when the weather is windy and your serve is affected – not to mention during matches in which your opponent slows the game down in an effort to break your momentum. In these situations, you have to learn to ignore your mistakes as you attempt to grind out a win.

The third requirement in dealing with setbacks is that you need a toolbox of practical *mistake-management techniques* which can be used when things go wrong. These techniques are designed to help you to let go of errors so that you don't dwell on them unnecessarily. Using these techniques prevents us from engaging in 'snowballing' – a form of chained thinking in which we allow one negative idea to trigger another one like a snowball rolling downhill.[5] A typical snowball thought is something like, 'If I miss a tackle early in the game, I always play badly.' This thought could make you so anxious that you concede a foul in your first challenge of the match – which might then cause you to lose confidence and 'hide' on the pitch. The main benefit of mistake-management techniques is that they stop the 'snowball' from gathering momentum not only by preventing you from indulging in fortune telling but also by helping you to re-focus on the present. Effective mistake-management skills are crucial at all levels of competitive sport. Later in the chapter, we'll provide some practical tips to help you in this aspect of your game.

Before we finish this section, however, it's important to point out that mistakes contribute to the dramatic appeal of competitive sport. In fact, you could argue that from a spectator's perspective, the real drama of watching top sports stars in action comes not from admiring their robotic perfection but from anticipating how they will react to setbacks during the event itself. This insight leads us to the obvious question – why are setbacks inevitable in sport?

Prepare to make mistakes

Everyone makes mistakes. For example, consider the following mishaps by top-level athletes.

Whoops!

- Tennis star Roger Federer, who has won more grand slam singles titles than any other player in history, served *three consecutive double faults* when defeated by Andy Murray in the 2012 Shanghai Masters tournament – a mistake that rarely happens even to a novice.[6]

> - The Ethiopian athlete Kenenisa Bekele (a 10,000m Olympic champion) famously lost a race because he actually *miscounted* the number of laps he had completed in the 2005 Boston Indoor Games. To explain, although indoor 3,000m races take place over 15 laps, Bekele raced for only 14 laps. Pausing after this lap in the mistaken belief that the race was over, he slowed down and allowed Ireland's Alistair Cragg to pass him and win the race.[7]
> - The American 50m rifle shooter Matthew Emmons squandered the opportunity to win a gold medal at the 2008 Olympic Games in Beijing when he inadvertently squeezed the trigger at the wrong time on his last shot.[8]

Why are mistakes inevitable in sport? At least three reasons spring to mind. To begin with, it's impossible to play flawlessly at all times because nobody's perfect. Even Muhammad Ali, one of the greatest athletes of all time, experienced defeats both *before* and *after* he became a world champion. Despite these setbacks, he never lost his confidence as a boxer because he knew that one loss doesn't make you a loser. In his own words,

> *'Only a man who knows what it is like to be defeated can reach down to the bottom of his soul and come up with the extra ounce of power it takes to win when the match is even.'*[9]

Second, as we've explained, the pressures and distractions of competition (see Chapters 4 and 5) induce errors among even the world's best performers. The third reason why mistakes abound in sport is because it's very difficult to anticipate the way in which opponents may play or react in a game – and errors can creep in as you try to adjust to what they're doing.

. . . But don't fear them!

Although it's important to strive for a perfect performance every time you play sport, it is very unhelpful to castigate yourself for failing to achieve it. Nevertheless, some people set impossibly high standards for themselves all the time. Let's explore this issue in more detail.

'Perfectionism' involves two separate but related dispositions – a tendency to set an excessively high standard for your own performance and a habit of criticising yourself harshly for failing to achieve it. Underlying these unhealthy dispositions lies an uncompromising 'all or nothing' belief – the toxic assumption that if you don't perform perfectly all of the time, you're a failure. There is no middle ground for the perfectionist.

As you might expect, perfectionism in thinking can cause lots of problems for you as an athlete. For example, it encourages you to associate mistakes with failure and to become preoccupied with avoiding errors at all costs. Also, by encouraging you to dwell on your mistakes, perfectionism makes you lose sight of the skills that you performed well in a given sport situation. In other words, perfectionism prevents you from seeing the big picture.

Not surprisingly, the more extreme your level of perfectionism, the less tolerance you will show for even the most trivial of errors. The result of this excessive emphasis on mistakes is that perfectionist performers end up being motivated more by a *fear of failure* rather than by the hope of success. Accordingly, perfectionism usually triggers anxiety. Put simply, people who are scared of making mistakes tend to become unusually nervous in competitive situations and their performance suffers a result. Again, in the words of Muhammad Ali,

> *'He who is not prepared to take risks will accomplish nothing in life.'*[10]

So, the lesson is clear. Take risks and be prepared to make mistakes. Let's now turn to the question of how mistakes affect people's performance in sport.

How mistakes affect your behaviour in sport

Mistakes affect athletes in a number of ways – some obvious, others more subtle. On the obvious side, they can alter the result of a sporting contest. For example, if your football or hockey team concedes a needless penalty kick in injury time in a match where the scores are level, you are likely to lose the game. Less obviously, mistakes affect the way in which athletes think, feel and behave in competitive situations.

1. How you think

To begin with, mistakes can make you think differently about your game. If you make a bad blunder early in a match, you may decide that it's not your day and begin to imagine that other mistakes will surely follow. This kind of superstitious thinking (sometimes called fortune telling) is very common in sport. Often, the first link in the chain of such thinking is negative 'self-talk' – the little voice inside our heads that scolds us for making mistakes ('That's rubbish – you're playing like a loser'). Research suggests that top players have developed mistake-management skills that enable them to ignore such unhelpful self-criticism and focus instead on planning what to do next. This approach is illustrated clearly by the golfer Pádraig Harrington who observed,

> *'I know I can't swing it well every day but there is no reason why I can't think well every day.'*[11]

2. How you feel

Mistakes can also affect you emotionally by denting your confidence and making you feel frustrated and angry. Indeed, of all the emotional reactions caused by mistakes, anger is probably the most commonly experienced. So, how does this emotion affect your performance in sport?

Although anger may have certain short-term physical benefits (e.g., it can temporarily increase your strength and intensity), it actually *impairs* rather than enhances athletic performance. This is especially true in sports (such as snooker, shooting, golf and tennis) that require precise eye–hand coordination, fine perceptual judgement and delicate motor movements. In such sports, anger is usually counter-productive. To illustrate this point, two unusual examples of self-directed anger spring to mind. First, in the 1940s, an American professional golfer named Lefty Stackhouse actually punched himself for making a mistake on the course.[12] More recently, Mikhail Youzhny, the Russian tennis player, was so incensed by an unforced error in a match against Nicolas Almagro that he smashed his racquet against his head – drawing blood![13]

As you might expect, winners in sport tend to have an emotional profile characterised by lower levels of anger and depression when compared with less successful counterparts. This is known as the iceberg profile[14] because negative mood scores are all below the average (or water), while the score for vigour or physical intensity is above the water. Despite this discovery, the sporting community has a rather ambivalent attitude to anger. For example, fans who flock to see John McEnroe playing on the Seniors tennis tour expect to witness him losing his temper. They may even believe that in his prime, he seemed to play *better* tennis when venting his anger on court than when calm. Unfortunately, research suggests exactly the opposite conclusion. To explain, there is compelling evidence that expressing your anger simply makes you *angrier* rather than more productive.[15] This finding raises an important question for players and coaches. Does reducing your anger impair your competitive performance in sport?

Many coaches are wary of curbing athletes' displays of anger in case it lowers their drive and performance on the field of play. For example, after the England soccer star Wayne Rooney had been sent off for stamping on Ricardo Carvalho in the 2006 World Cup quarter-final match against Portugal, Sven-Göran Eriksson (England's manager at the time) remarked that,

> '*Of course, he has a temperament (sic) but you have to live with that. You can't take that away from him because he would never be the same player.*'[16]

Similar views were expressed by Ronnie O'Sullivan, the brilliant but mercurial snooker player. He claimed that venting your emotions is a good thing in sport because it shows your 'character'. Indeed, after he had been criticised for making an obscene gesture at the 2004 Embassy World Championship, O'Sullivan said,

> '*I'll keep showing my feelings by swearing and gesturing . . . I'm not switching off my emotions for anyone and if I swear at a pocket while playing it's because I'm annoyed and showing some character. What's wrong with that?*'[17]

Well, to answer this rhetorical question, all we have to do is to explore some case studies of athletes whose performance actually *improved* when they learned to curb their temper. For example, consider the case of Bjorn Borg, the former tennis star with the ice-cool temperament who won 11 grand slam titles in his career. It may surprise you to discover that he had been an extremely angry and volatile player in his early years:

> 'When I was twelve, I behaved badly on court, swearing, cheating, throwing rackets – so my club suspended me for six months. When I came back, I didn't open my mouth . . . I felt that I played my best tennis being focused.'[18]

Clearly, as this quotation reveals, Borg wasn't always as cool as the iceberg that he became in later years! What his remarkable story tells us is that with proper self-control, hot anger can be turned into cool concentration.

3. How you behave

The third way in which mistakes affect athletes is by influencing their behaviour during a game. For example, a soccer player who makes a silly mistake in a match may subsequently hide on the pitch, avoiding passes from team-mates or shirking defensive or attacking responsibilities. Based on such experience, many players have developed informal strategies which (they hope) will correct this problem. For example, some people try to wipe out a mistake by taking a decisive action immediately afterwards. Unfortunately, this 'over compensation' effect is well known in sport because it usually leads to even *bigger* problems. For example, according to Keith Wood, the former Ireland and Lions rugby captain:

Bjorn Borg (Courtesy of Inpho Photography)

'There was a time when, if I made an error, I wanted to immediately make up for it by doing something spectacular. Inevitably, I would make a further error and compound the situation. Now I have developed a routine whereby I repeat a mantra word to myself. This clears my mind, and I then focus on next doing a simple thing well.'[19]

In summary, this section has shown you that mistakes affect what players think, feel and do in competitive situations. Let's see how we can apply this knowledge now to help Alan, a fictitious badminton player, to react better to the errors that he makes on court.

Mistake management in action

Alan is an extremely talented young badminton player who has recently been selected for the national elite squads for his age group. Unfortunately, his volatile temperament is holding him back from making further progress. This flaw is obvious in Alan's reaction to mistakes. For example, Michael, his coach, has noticed that when Alan makes an unforced error, his first reaction is to throw his racket on the ground or to hit the net. This display of temper has not only earned him penalty points in several national tournaments but also puts him in the wrong frame of mind for the next point during games. Michael is also worried about how frequently Alan criticises himself aloud and uses swear words on court – reactions that send all the wrong messages to his opponents. After some advice from a sport psychologist, Michael tries to replace Alan's faulty habits with the following mistake-management strategies on court.

Whenever he makes an error, Alan imitates or 'shadows' the shot that he should have played. This helps him to correct the mistake and override the memory of it when he prepares to play a similar shot later in the game.

Another mistake management used by Alan is to acknowledge the mistake, turn his back on it to symbolise putting it in the past, and then turn around again to face his opponent, either to serve or receive.

Finally, Alan has been taught to release his frustration after a mistake either by standing still for a moment or by smiling. This helps to defuse his tension and annoyance.

The latest news about Alan is that he's working very hard on his game and has become a lot more consistent on court. He's still prone to losing his temper from time to time but overall, Alan and the national coach are very pleased with his progress.

Putting it behind you

Earlier in the chapter, we explained that even the best athletes make mistakes. But errors, by themselves, are rarely decisive in any sport. What really matters is how quickly and efficiently you can put your mistake behind you and *get on with the game*. As the former champion golfer Gary Player remarked,

> 'the toughest thing for people to learn in golf is to accept bad holes and then to forget about them.'[20]

Clearly, the way in which you react to mistakes says a lot about your character. For example, imagine that you're a footballer and you lose the ball in a tackle with an opponent. Do you wave your hands and appeal to the referee for a foul – or do you track back immediately and try to retrieve the ball from the opposing player? Clearly, in such little incidents, a player's mental toughness is revealed. Let's now turn to the question of how you can you use your errors as feedback to improve your game.

Using mistakes to improve your game: Asking the right questions

A key theme of this chapter is that mistakes provide feedback for the prepared mind. But in order to benefit from the feedback that errors provide, you must be able to analyse them. Proper analysis requires you to ask yourself a series of incisive questions to pinpoint precisely which aspect of your game let you down – and, perhaps more importantly, why.

To learn from setbacks, you need to understand four key components of athletic performance – physical, technical, tactical and psychological. First, the physical side of your performance refers to concepts like fitness, strength and stamina that can be measured objectively. The technical side involves your level of skill or proficiency in your chosen sport. Next, we have the tactical dimension that refers to your awareness of the strategic aspects of your game. Included here are such skills as planning and decision making. Finally, the psychological aspect of your performance refers to your mental fitness for competitive action – what we cover in this book.

Asking the right questions about your performance is the best way to begin to analyse your mistakes. It also provides a natural follow-up to the skills outlined in Chapter 3.

Analysing your mistakes

If you play any sport, including golf, it is important to review your performance regularly. One of the best ways of doing this is to ask the following questions about your mistakes.

1. What exactly happened when I made the error?

The more precisely you can answer this question the better. For example, the statement 'I missed' is less helpful than 'I judged the distance of my putt wrongly and it fell short of the hole'.

2. When did my mistake happen?

For example, did your putting let you down as you got more tired towards the end of the round? If so, then it may be helpful to note that 'I missed four short putts over the last seven holes'.

3. What was the result of my mistake?

Usually, this consequence can be described quite easily. For example, 'I lost two shots on that hole because I three-putted from a short distance'.

4. How did I react to the mistake?

A common reaction is to let the mistake linger in your mind so that it prevents you from playing properly afterwards. In this case, you might note that 'I got angry with myself and couldn't keep my mistake out of my mind as I played the next few holes'.

5. What parts of my game (physical, technical, tactical or psychological) should I review?

If your errors tend to happen in the last few holes, then perhaps you need to work on your physical fitness as well as your concentration.

Developing the right attitude to mistakes: The good, the bad and the ugly

Mistakes in sport tend to elicit a variety of reactions from athletes. These reactions include the good (trying to learn from them), the bad (fortune telling – seeing them as pre-determined; mentioned earlier in this chapter) and the ugly (losing emotional control through angry behaviour).

Interestingly, the renowned tennis coach Brad Gilbert coined the phrase 'winning ugly' to describe the strategy of grinding out results by doing whatever is necessary in order to secure a victory.[21] Borrowing from Gilbert, we've coined the phrase 'losing ugly'.

Losing ugly: The worst reaction to mistakes

For us, 'losing ugly' is the worst way of reacting to mistakes because it regards them as signs of inescapable failure in the future. In other words, you may believe that if you make a blunder, you're doomed. By contrast, a more helpful way to look at setbacks is to regard them as temporary outcomes of a set of circumstances that can change. In our experience, a key characteristic of persistent, highly motivated people is that they see failure as a form of feedback that indicates those things that need to be changed in their lives. This attitude gives them the 'courage to fail' that we mentioned earlier. And because successful people are not afraid to fail, they take the risks that constitute the building blocks of progress and improvement.

Because mistakes make us feel uncomfortable, we rarely like to talk about them. But we can't make progress without making mistakes and analysing why they happened. Indeed, as we hinted at earlier in this chapter, if you haven't experienced setbacks, you're being denied the opportunity to learn and improve. As Clive Woodward, coach of the England rugby team that won the 2003 World Cup, remarked,

> *'In order to win, you have to know how to lose. You have to know how to handle your setbacks in order to move forward.'*[22]

The lesson is clear – to make progress, you must have the courage to fail.

Do you have that courage?

Mistakes challenge you to improve your game and a key step in this process is having the 'courage to fail'. Interestingly, Frank Dick, the former British national athletics coach, claims that when such courage is missing, people 'play safe' and invariably perform below their ability.[23] In his view, the fear of making mistakes is probably the biggest barriers to athletes' efforts to fulfil their potential. This fear stunts people's growth because it prevents them from taking risks. And without risk-taking, there can be no progress. But as well as having the courage to fail, it's important to be able to 'frame' your mistakes in a helpful way if you want to learn from them.

Framing your mistakes

As we've explained, most athletes are uncomfortable about discussing their mistakes. They tend to regard them as personal weaknesses which are embarrassing and hence should be hidden rather than confronted. But there is another way of looking at setbacks – one that allows you to learn from them. This idea is echoed by the coaching motto that it's okay for players to make mistakes – as long as they don't make the same ones over and over again! This is also what the playwright Samuel Beckett meant when he urged people to 'try again, fail again'.

Some practical tips on reframing your setbacks are listed in the box below.

Reframing your setbacks: Eight practical tips

1. Stop taking failure so personally. Everyone makes mistakes – but not everyone blames themselves as a result.
2. Try to put your disappointments in perspective: In a year's time, you probably won't even remember why you were so upset about some silly mistake.
3. Stop torturing yourself about what might have been. Wishful (or 'counter-factual') thinking can't change anything so it's a waste of time.
4. Stop focusing on the mistake you made: Concentrate instead on what you plan to do differently the next time the situation arises.
5. Try to learn from the way in which other people (especially consistent winners) handle setbacks: You'll probably find that successful people try hard not to make the same mistake twice.
6. Ask yourself what advice you'd give someone else who made a similar mistake to your one: It's surprising how objective we can be when we're looking at other people's problems.
7. Ask yourself what aspects of the setback are due to factors that can change in the future: Usually, successful people regard setbacks as events caused by things that they can change in time.
8. Try to identify at least one good thing (e.g., a lesson learned such as a change in perspective, a resolve to work harder on your game) that happened as a result of your setback.

So, what are the good and the bad ways of looking at mistakes in sport? Perhaps the best way to answer this question is by exploring what research tells us about how we try to make sense of things that happen in our lives.

Explaining your mistakes: Why it's important to look on the bright side!

Most of us are interested in seeking explanations for the things that go wrong in our lives. Interestingly, research shows that the way in which you make sense of things that happened to you in the past (i.e., your attributional style, see Chapter 2) can affect your chances of achieving success in the future. For example, consider two different ways of explaining the cause of a particular result. On the one hand, a badminton player may attribute her victory over an opponent to her own fighting spirit on court.

This is a motivational explanation for the result. By contrast, the manager of a defeated football team may attribute a specific result to bad luck (e.g., the winning goal was a deflection) or to some other misfortune over which he had no control

Badminton player (Courtesy of iStockphoto)

(e.g., an apparently unfair refereeing decision). These examples show different attributional approaches in action. On the one hand, the badminton player's explanation for her victory invoked an internal, personal quality (her determination), on the other hand the football manager's explanation referred to external factors (bad luck and/or poor refereeing).

Building on our discussion in Chapter 2 of what makes the winning mind in sport, research shows that people have a tendency to favour a similar way of explaining things that happen to them in different situations in their lives. This style can be measured using a questionnaire called the 'Attributional Style Questionnaire' (ASQ) that requires you to identify the possible causes of various hypothetical situations.[24] An interesting feature of this test is that it also asks you to rate these causes along three separate dimensions:

1. **Locus of causality** (Did I cause this event or was it caused by someone else?).
2. **Stability of causality** (Is the cause likely to persist in the future or not?).
3. **Globality of causality** (Is the cause likely to affect every aspect of my life or not?).

By analysing the pattern of your responses to the ASQ, two different attributional styles – pessimistic and optimistic – can be identified. In general, pessimists tend to explain setbacks in ways that are personal ('it was my fault'), permanent ('this situation is always going to be like this and there's very little I can do to change it') and far-reaching ('this failure has ruined almost every aspect of my life') whereas optimists tend to see them as being temporary and situation-specific.

Research also reveals that winners in sport tend to provide rather different explanations for their success than do losers.[25] Typically, winners tend to favour attributions to internal and personally controllable factors such as the amount of practice that they've engaged in before the event. Remarkably, these attributions can help to predict the likelihood of actual athletic success in the future. To apply this idea, imagine that you're a young sprinter who is perplexed by a series of poor results in races recently. If you develop the habit of attributing these poor results to a lack of *ability* (a relatively stable internal factor) rather than to the high quality of your competitors (a variable external factor), then you may lose confidence in yourself and give up your sport.

Swimming against the tide

Researchers administered the ASQ to collegiate swimmers prior to the start of their competitive season.[26] Before the start of the swimming season, Seligman and his team gave the test to 50 swimmers in a university. Then, they rated each of the swimmers on how they thought they were likely to perform over the season. Three main findings emerged.

1. Swimmers with a pessimistic explanatory style were more likely to perform below the level of coaches' expectations during the season than were swimmers with a more optimistic outlook. In fact, the pessimists on the ASQ had about twice as many unexpectedly poor swims as did their optimistic colleagues.
2. Pessimistic swimmers were less likely to 'bounce back' from simulated defeats than were optimistic counterparts. This result emerged after a rigged defeat (manipulated by providing false feedback, e.g., swimmers were told that their swim-times were slower by up to five seconds than they actually were); the performance of pessimistic swimmers deteriorated whereas that of relative optimists did not.
3. The explanatory style scores of the swimmers were significantly predictive of swimming performance even after coaches' judgements of ability to overcome a setback had been removed from the analysis.

Given the importance of explanatory style in sport, now let's see whether you're an optimist or a pessimist.

Is the glass half full or half empty?

In order to find out if you're an optimist or a pessimist, let's ask you some questions.

Q1. Think of a match that you lost recently. Do you think that you were personally responsible for the result or was it due to some external circumstances? This question relates to 'personalisation' (i.e., an internal or external cause).

Q2. Do you think that the cause of this result will persist in the future?

Q3. How much will this event affect other areas of your life? This question assesses the pervasiveness of the cause. The more aspects of your life you think will be affected, the more pervasive is the cause in question.

Analysis

If you attributed the event to yourself (Q1) and to factors which will not change in the future (Q2) and if you believe that the cause affects many different aspects of your life (Q3), then you probably have a *pessimistic* explanatory style. If so, then you tend explain setbacks by saying 'I've only myself to blame' (personalisation), 'It's going to happen again and again' (permanence) and 'It's going to ruin my whole life' (pervasiveness).

In general, pessimists believe that negative experiences are their fault, will never change and are catastrophic. Optimists, on the other hand, tend to interpret setbacks as being caused by temporary circumstances which can be changed in the future – given sufficient effort on their part.

Can you change your approach?

We hope that by now you will have thought long and hard about your preferred attributional style. You can *change* this style, however, by learning to think differently about what may have caused your setbacks. For example, imagine that you're a golf coach who wants to help players to become more self-reliant. To do so, you could train them to change their attributions as follows. Let's say that one of your female golfers confides in you after a match that she was lucky to get away with a shot that barely skimmed the rim of the bunker before landing on the green. Picking up what she said, you could try to replace her attribution to an *external unstable* factor (luck) with one to an 'internal' factor (e.g., 'If I concentrate on getting more uplift on my sand shots, I will become a much better bunker player'). In the long term, this attribution to a practice factor will motivate her to work hard at her game. Remember – winners are workers, only losers make excuses.

At this stage, let's summarise some key ideas from this chapter in the form of practical tips on mistake management.

Five practical tips on mistake management

From the beginning, we've emphasised the importance of putting mistakes and misfortune behind you as quickly and as efficiently as possible. The reason we place such importance on this mental skill is that competitive sport is full of examples of sports teams and individuals who recovered from seemingly impossible deficits to win crucial matches.[27] To illustrate, in rugby, Leinster won the 2011 Heineken Cup final by defeating Northampton (33-22) despite being 22-6 down at half-time. Similarly, in 2010, Fiji came back from 28-0 down to defeat Tonga 41-38 in the Pacific Nations Cup. In soccer, Liverpool famously defeated AC Milan in a penalty shoot-out in the 2005 Champions' League final even though they had been 3-0 down at half-time. Another memorable comeback was staged by Dennis Taylor who won the world snooker championship in 1985 (by 18-17) despite trailing Steve Davis by 8 frames to 0 at one stage. More recently, in a soccer World Cup qualifying match in 2012, Sweden fought back from a 4-0 deficit against Germany to draw the game by scoring 4 goals in the last 30 minutes. Inspired by such recoveries from adversity, here are five practical tips on positive mistake management.

Managing mistakes: Five practical tips

1. Try to learn from your mistakes – don't ignore them. Most athletes think that if they ignore their mistakes, they will go away. This is not true because mistakes stem mainly from habits which will re-surface if not corrected.
2. Don't be too hard on yourself when you make a mistake.
3. Keep a log of one thing that you're proud of and one thing that you need to work harder on (e.g., correcting a mistake) after every competitive game. By identifying patterns in your errors over time, you'll be able to seek advice from coaches about how to improve your technical skills.
4. Observe how top athletes in your sport deal with their mistakes and try to learn from them.
5. Develop a short mistake-management routine for your sport so that you can put your errors behind you.

The last word

In this chapter, we explained that in order to achieve athletic success, you must be able to put your setbacks and mistakes behind you and simply 'get on with it'. We began by showing you how to develop a helpful way of 'framing', or looking constructively at, things that go wrong for you in sport so that you can either learn from them or use them to motivate you in some way. After that, we provided some practical tips on developing effective mistake-management techniques. Moving from theory to practice, let's leave the last word on handling mistakes to the golfer Pádraig Harrington:

> 'Unless you're prepared to make mistakes and put your head on the line, you're going to get nothing and it'll be worth nothing . . . You will have many mistakes and failures and the higher up you get, the more magnified those failures will be. But they're all worth it in the end because when the good days come, they're made all the better by the memory of those mistakes and failures . . . If you're looking for average, then try not to make mistakes but if you're looking to be great, you've got to make loads of mistakes.'[28]

8   The team

Until now our journey through sport psychology has focused exclusively on the *individual* and how to harness personal mental skills. Undoubtedly, this work is core to sport psychology and yet individual activity represents only a small part of the story because sport is, at heart, *social*. With this in mind, this chapter will head in a slightly different direction, aimed at exploring the dynamics of sport teams. While previous chapters were directed towards self-improvement, here we aim to present material that will be of practical benefit especially to those who manage, coach or captain teams, to help understand the workings of teams and thereby improve performance. For those who have particular team problems to deal with right now, we recommend that you read this chapter in conjunction with the relevant 'Team performance: Problems and solutions' section on p. 178, where we address specific team issues head on.

By their very nature, a great many sports are based on teamwork and the complex interactions between individual members. However, even solitary athletic endeavours (such as marathon running, skiing or sailing) rarely fail to involve teams in some shape or form. Take golf, at first glance the archetype of an individual sporting pursuit – just you and the golf course – but first impressions can be deceptive. On closer inspection, we find that top golfers are rarely alone; they travel and work with a large support team of advisors including caddies, managers, agents, physiotherapists, swing coaches, putting specialists – and psychologists, and on occasions such as the Ryder Cup, they actually play as a team.

Therefore popular portrayals of the solitary athlete can be misleading because behind the scenes there will normally be a team involved in setting the person off down the road – and then keeping them on track. The solo long-distance sailor Ellen MacArthur is the first to acknowledge that her single-handed voyages across the world's oceans were based on teamwork, involving a constant exchange of information with her shore team before, during and after each challenge. Her words, at the news conference after breaking the single-handed round-the-world record, speak volumes for the role played by her team:

> *'A record is nothing if not shared. I'm proud of the record but I'm even more proud to be working with the best team in the world. When I was out there I was never ever alone, there was always a team of people behind me, in mind if not in body.'*[1]

In most sports, teamwork is seen as something to be encouraged and it is difficult to bring to mind many sports where this is not the case. In view of the significance of teamwork, it is right and proper that we should turn our attention away from the individual and towards the collective – to see how individual talent and potential can be drawn together effectively within a team context.

What is a team?

It would be too easy to gloss over this question. After all, we have experience of teams throughout our lives – but what actually defines a 'team' and more critically, is our confidence in teams (e.g., 'There's safety in numbers'; 'Two heads are better than one'; 'Many hands make light work') really justified?

To be frank, our experience with teams in many sports suggests it is rare for them to bring out the best in everyone if they are left to their own devices. On the contrary, time and again we encounter teams littered with unhelpful social influences that can interfere with individual performance. As one classic example, research consistently shows that when people work together on a common task, unconsciously they will generate *less* total effort than when working alone – a phenomenon known as 'social loafing' (see p. 140). Despite such evidence, our unwavering faith in teams remains unshaken. With this caution in mind, let's first explore what teams are, before considering what they could become.

While we may all 'know' what a team is, this casual experience is no substitute for careful analysis of the qualities that make teams good, bad or just plain ugly.

Winning team (Courtesy of University College Dublin)

In the literature, you will find teams defined by five features – interaction, structure, cohesion, goals and identity.[2] Almost any sport team, from the most organised professional club to the most casual outfit, will normally qualify on all five counts – but sometimes only just.

When trying to work out what has gone wrong with a team, these features actually offer a really useful starting point for judging strengths and weaknesses. To show what we mean, think of a team you've been involved with, and then reflect on the following.

Understanding your team

Interaction

During play: Do the players communicate effectively? What interferes with effective communication? Is communication generally positive or negative? Who talks and who listens? Is body language positive or negative?

In the changing room: Do team members talk openly? Are they generally quiet or vocal? Who takes the lead? Who makes useful contributions? Is there much banter and how is it taken?

During training: How do team members interact during training? Who speaks and who doesn't, and with whom? Do players volunteer information freely?

Socially: Do the team mix socially – where, when and how frequently? Who socialises and who doesn't? Are there cliques? Do younger and older players mix freely? Who takes the lead and who follows?

Overall, how would you score the team on interaction? _____ (out of 10)

Structure

How long has the team been together? Are there well-defined team roles, both formal and informal? Has the team 'matured' as a working unit? Are those with assigned roles (e.g., captain, vice-captain) good communicators? Who is respected? Who is listened to? Who cracks jokes? Who is usually the centre of affairs? Is there a pecking order within the team? Are the team punctual? Is attendance at training good or patchy?

Overall, how would you score the team on structure? _____ (out of 10)

Task cohesion

As a team, would an observer say they play 'together'? Does the team seem to bring out the best in individual players? Do they give the impression during play itself that they know what to do and how to do it as a unit? Would you describe them as a 'tight' team on the pitch? Is training competitive – is there a healthy edge or are they relaxed?

Overall, how would you score the team on task cohesion? _____ (out of 10)

Social cohesion

Off the pitch, are they a tight group? Are they respectful of each other? Are they exclusive? Do they seem comfortable in each other's company? Are they too comfortable? Do they choose to socialise together?

Overall, how would you score the team on social cohesion? _____ (out of 10)

Goals

Has the team well-defined short, medium and long-term goals? Are they implicit or explicit? Does everyone always seem to pull in the same direction? Are there different agendas at work in the team? Are there dissenting voices or whispers either within the team or among the backroom staff? Does the team stay 'on message' during a game? Is the collective goal stronger than individual goals or priorities? How committed are they to the cause?

Overall, how would you score the team on goals? _____ (out of 10)

Identity

Does the team have an identity (e.g., has it defined its strengths and weaknesses)? Is the team defined by its own qualities or those of others? Is the history of the club or previous teams a help or a hindrance in terms of the team's own identity? Do the key players (e.g., captain) reinforce the identity of the team through what they do and what they say?

Overall, how would you score the team on identity? _____ (out of 10)

By carefully reflecting on your answers, you can start building a team profile and begin to really understand what makes the team tick, while probably becoming aware that the term cohesion or team spirit is more complex than you may have imagined. *Task cohesion* is concerned with how well the team works together as a playing unit while *social cohesion* is about how well they get on together socially. These are independent factors and should never be confused – one definitely predicts success, the other is often predicted by success. No prizes for guessing which is which.

Before going any further, it is worth remembering that no two teams will ever be the same – or should ever *try* to be the same. In practical terms, this means the management of every team must be tailored to the particular qualities of those individuals. To illustrate, one team may have a strong sense of identity, clear, explicit and well-formulated goals, well-defined structures and yet interaction between players is poor and the team lacks both task and social cohesion. Another team may communicate well and task cohesion may be strong yet its sense of identity may be poorly developed and different motives or agendas may be driving individual members towards very different goals. Without labouring the point, it is worth spending time exploring the precise qualities of the group of players with whom you are working before moving forwards too hastily.

The looking glass

Taking these five team dimensions into consideration, you can begin to reflect on the qualities of the team itself (see Chapter 3). At this stage avoid the temptation of labelling the team crudely as being either 'good' or 'poor'. Instead, try to be more precise in defining the various strengths and weaknesses before you. Only through a systematic evaluation of each one of the five elements will you produce a solid foundation for later work.

Also, be aware that even within one team there may well be several sub-units or teams and especially whenever a common goal is not shared or task cohesion is weak. As one example, the bench and the court teams in sports such as basketball may operate to different agendas and may respond quite differently to successes and failures. For example, if you are a substitute and the player that you are supposed to replace is having such a great game that you aren't required, how will you feel?

Carlos Tevez arguing with Mancini (Courtesy of Inpho Photography)

Sport is littered with stories of the tensions between the starting team and the bench, some heavily publicised, others still waiting to be told!

Even *within* a starting team there may be different dynamics depending on each position and role. Within a rugby team, for example, the climate that is needed to optimise the performance of backs and forwards may differ. Forwards must work together as a collective while backs may be given more space for creativity and flair.

In a related way, the extent of each players' role clarity or how well-defined their job is within the team will have a different impact on performance depending on the position in question. With defensive roles, role clarity will usually relate positively with performance. In other words, you need to know what to do and how to do it in order to perform as part of an organised and effective unit. By contrast, attacking roles may suggest a negative relationship between role clarity and performance where too much clarity actually inhibits creativity and flair. In other words being told precisely what you have to do is unlikely to help you find that elusive key for unlocking a resolute defence.

So, a reflection on roles and role clarity cannot ignore group dynamics and must take into account factors including playing position, as well as the players' temperaments. With this in mind, you can see why so many players who managers would describe as 'difficult' are those in positions where role conflict goes hand in hand with creativity and good performance. The soccer legend George Best is one example of a creative, attacking genius who ran rings around defenders and team managers with equal dexterity.

George Best (Courtesy of Inpho Photography)

The team in its place

Having developed a profile of the team, the next step is to consider the circumstances in which the team performs. These include demands made by the particular sport and also the environment in which the team must operate. To help understand these issues, the following three questions may help.

First, does the sport involve activity that is *unitary* (where the task cannot be broken down and where group members typically work together on a single task, e.g., a rowing eight) or is it *divisible* (where the task can be broken down to smaller units and where each team member can be assigned to particular tasks, e.g., a horse riding team or sailing crew)?

Second, in which ways does team performance relate to *quantity* or *quality* of contribution? Some sports emphasise quantity of contribution (known as *maximisation* tasks, e.g., tug-of-war, weightlifting) while some focus on greater quality of contribution (*optimisation* tasks, e.g., snooker, darts, shooting, golf). Very generally, the former usually involve gross motor skills whereas the latter depend on fine motor coordination. In the real world, every sport combines the two, to some degree, but being sensitive to the quantity/quality ratio in your sport can be helpful in deciding the climate or atmosphere that will maximise the chances of team success.

Third, does the team performance depend on what is called interaction or co-action? On the one hand there are *interactive sports* involving coordination between team members (e.g., soccer, rugby, netball, basketball, hockey) while on the other hand there are *co-active sports* that involve team members performing individually but in a team context (e.g., golf, bowls, archery, skiing, shooting, darts, snooker). Very few sports are exclusively one or the other. Instead, almost all sports combine unique interactive and co-active elements through different phases of play. Sports such as baseball or cricket are intriguing in this way as both demand high levels of both co-action and interaction. For example, fielding is principally an interactive team activity but batting and bowling are primarily, but not exclusively, co-active.

Bearing this complex mix between the individual and the team endeavour in mind, it is probably no coincidence that certain players in both baseball and cricket have been renowned as exceptional individual performers – but ones who never quite made the grade when it came to the team element of the game. To illustrate, the following extract is taken from the official English cricket website describing one of the greatest English batsmen of all times, Geoffrey Boycott:

> '*As opener he saw his first task as scoring heavily enough to protect his teams against defeat, and in Test cricket and the County Championship – the matches that counted in the first-class averages – he was as sparing with the attacking strokes as, in retirement, he is strident in his opinions on the game. How valuable he was to England is shown by the fact that only 20 of his 108 Tests ended in defeat, mainly when he failed. . . . . . A loner, and an insatiable net-player, he was short of friends inside the game; indeed there were many who heartily disliked him because of his self-centredness.*'[3]

Boycott may not have won many plaudits as a team player but as a batsman he was second to none and his contribution to England's team performance was immense.

As sports differ so widely in their nature so it is inevitable that the significance of team factors in determining success will also vary. Not surprisingly the more that a sport requires team members to interact (*interactive sports*) then the more significant that team cohesion is likely to be. In sports where athletes may represent the same team but individual performance does not depend on teamwork (*co-acting sports*) then cohesion will be less significant. Some sports may be both highly interactive and co-active (e.g., rowing, tug-of-war) whereas some may be highly interactive but involve less identifiable co-action (e.g., volleyball). Others may be low on both dimensions (e.g., marathon running, chess) and yet others may be co-active but not interactive (e.g., archery, bowls).

Reflecting on all three questions in combination, it becomes obvious that the team atmosphere and general dynamic that is likely to maximise performance will vary dramatically between sports. Never imagine that there is a simple formula for success or that the formula remains constant. Instead, at any moment the team character must reflect the particular demands of the situation and the key to success will often lie in identifying or profiling the circumstance and then tailoring the team to these demands.

Successful teams: Fit for purpose

To summarise what we have said so far, there is no such thing as a 'good' team – but there are teams that are *fit for purpose*, in the sense that they are equipped to meet the demands of their particular sport and the challenges that come their way. As a broad foundation for success, a team that is fit for purpose should aspire to create an environment where individual players can flourish and express their individual talents, and where the team's performance becomes greater than the sum of its parts. Great teams, and great managers, do more than simply bring together talented individuals; they bring '*value-addedness*' and are able to create performances that are greater than an objective assessment of individual players and their talents would suggest are possible.

Realising both these aspirations presents a challenge of considerable proportions for any coach or manager, especially as research suggests that small groups rarely perform at the level of their average member let alone their best member. It is here that good team management becomes critical. We'll deal with the mechanics of team management in Chapter 9 but for now it is important to recognise that management should not just be about setting and reaching *performance* targets but should also prioritise nurturing *satisfaction* with the team process or dynamic. Short-term performance is important (and in many professional sports is the only guarantee of continued employment for a manager) but without the extra 'value-added' factor, longer-term loyalty, and performance, will suffer. Most well-managed teams are characterised by a healthy balance between a concern for team performance and for team satisfaction. Let either one of these factors dominate and the well-being of the team will suffer.

Imagine teams in your chosen sport that have achieved success. Now consider both what they have in common and what makes them different. Very often you will find no common themes or profiles emerging. Each team faced its own distinctive challenges and met these in unique ways. As with the elusive search for a profile of the individual champion, it's not surprising that the team literature has struggled to find a winning team formula. Instead it has been able to identify critical variables that relate to success – and we have outlined these below.

Team cohesion

From an early age we learn to value teams and teamwork. As a consequence we soon develop beliefs about what makes a good team. High on this list is the idea that a tight, cohesive team is a good team and so coaches can feel that building a strong 'team spirit' is their number one priority. The world of popular sport constantly echoes and reinforces the significance of team spirit but often without taking stock of what this may actually mean – and when it can do more harm than good.

Successful teams will talk about the important role that team spirit has played in their success yet the jury is still out as to which one comes first. In other words, does team spirit create success or does success create this impression with the benefit of hindsight? Interestingly, the available research more strongly supports the second view – that success tends to breed team cohesion – but the impact of cohesion on success is much more debatable. Without doubt, task cohesion is critical – the team that plays and works together is the team that wins together. However, remember that task cohesion and social cohesion are distinct – the team that drinks together is not always the team that wins together but rest assured, they'll have lots of ways of explaining why they lost, over a pint!

Undoubtedly, if the team has bonded together around a common goal and with a common purpose, this will enhance commitment but the management of social cohesion should always be mindful of the dangers of too much and especially where this detracts from effective performance on the pitch.

Healthy conflict and rivalries within a team can often spur that team to success and individuals players to want to achieve great things. At times this philosophy has been taken to extremes. Take the example of Leicester Tigers Rugby Club, consistently one of the most successful teams in England and Europe. In their glory years in the 2000s, fights between players would appear to have been commonplace during training, if not even encouraged:

> 'The fascinating thing about Leicester is not so much the way they handle big games as how they behave in the privacy of their midweek practice sessions. The players all have different theories as to why the Tigers are hunting an unprecedented treble tomorrow but it is amazing how often conversation turns to training-ground fisticuffs. Welcome to a club whose idea of perfect harmony is to ensure players compete from dawn to dusk and, where necessary, punch one another's lights out.'[4]

In the words of a former captain, Martin Corry, these altercations were seen as a healthy sign of commitment,

> 'They're not something to be proud about but they show that people care. That's the most important thing.'[5]

Another danger attached to being a member of a 'tight team' is that this may encourage members to perform not to the best of their ability but the same as everyone else. The more cohesive the team, the less likely it may be that members will want to stand out and when the pressure comes on, the more likely it is that team members will turn inwards and seek comfort from their team-mates. This will not always help individual players to dig deep into their mental and physical resources but instead can make players feel comfortable and complacent with their mediocrity.

To effectively marry cohesion with success, our experience would suggest that certain positive steps have to be taken. First, team goals must be clearly defined. Second, expectations of individual players must be high; if goals are unclear and expectations are low or value is placed on solidarity at all costs (for example, not showing other players up), then performance will suffer. Third, the focus must rest squarely on task-related issues. Players may be different, with varied social lives and operating in diverse social worlds, and they should be allowed or even encouraged to be different away from the pitch or training ground. Remember, good teams thrive on difference, poor teams stifle individuality.

As one example, the (in)famous Wimbledon soccer team of the 1980s and 1990s ('The Crazy Gang') under manager Dave Bassett was presented to the outside world as a band of brothers, welded together at the hip through thick and thin, both on and off the pitch. Apparently, the reality was quite different, according to the personal accounts of former members of the 'gang'. Away from the training field and matches, they all went their separate ways – but when they played football, they played as one – and their results speak for themselves. They may not have been the prettiest of football teams to watch but they were pretty effective – largely due to a powerful shared sense of purpose and identity.

Team continuity and maturity

Any group or team will take time to develop into an effective working unit. It should come as no surprise to learn that research consistently shows a positive relationship between the length of time that a team plays together and its level of success – but only up to a point. Beyond that point, the climate that has developed in the team will influence whether the team continues to hunger for success or whether it starts to lose its cutting edge.

In the 1960s, an American psychologist called Bruce Tuckman unwittingly laid a false trail when he described group development as a series of orderly stages.[6] According to his model, the group initially gets together and works through the formal orientation stage (forming). Next, there may be heightened tension associated with competition for status and influence in the team (storming), before things settle down as norms, rules and standards of behaviour eventually stabilise (norming). Finally he argued that the group will have matured to a stage where it can work together as a unit (performing) and will continue to perform consistently until members finally go their separate ways (adjourning).

Clearly this process all takes time, and when players change, any group or team has to work through the process afresh and performance will invariably suffer during this period of readjustment. However, what the model fails to consider is what happens *beyond* very early stages of development – what climate will help a team to continue to perform well in the medium to long term, in other words, beyond norming?

Waving not drowning: Positive conflict

At this stage, we need to introduce another concept – *waving*. To explain, research suggests a stable team can become lazy or complacent and in these circumstances, team maturity and continuity can lead to underperformance. 'Waving' is about allowing healthy levels of conflict to ebb and flow in the team within defined limits. Knowing when to heat things up (thawing) and cool things down (freezing) is critical in developing the long-term health of the team but has often been ignored, at considerable cost.

As should be apparent by now, in the world of team sports conflict itself should never be thought of as a dirty word but as an essential ingredient in a healthy team. Hence conflict should never be avoided but must be *managed* effectively. Teams that function most positively are not those where everyone is going around continually supporting each other, patting each other on the back and discouraging dissent and nonconformity. Research shows that the most stable and productive teams are those where there is a healthy level of rivalry or conflict, where players can feel they can express their own opinions, where they can honestly and openly disagree with others, and where they have space to test their individual potential.

In contrast, the worst teams, whether in sport as in business, are usually those that try to eliminate conflict. In such situations, where disagreement is avoided at all costs, a phenomenon known as 'groupthink' can easily develop. Groupthink characterises groups where everyone is in agreement and where everyone strives hard to be like the others and agree with everyone else.[7] Teams that suffer from groupthink underperform and actively go out of their way to suppress difference and individual flair. Teams that avoid groupthink become comfortable with managed conflict and healthy rivalry between team members in an environment where people can be true to themselves without fear of being outlawed.

Team identity

Research confirms the common-sense view that a strong sense of identity, knowing who you are and what you are about, is closely tied to positive feelings of group solidarity, self-esteem and confidence. Many sport teams ignore this simple message at their cost. For example, instead of building a team around a strong sense of who or what they are, the temptation can be to borrow an identity from another team, club or nation, or to rely on history repeating itself in the club colours of old. In these circumstances, history can become a burden and especially where the new team differs in critical ways from its predecessors, including its style of play.

According to one commentator, Sid Lowe, a long established, powerful and positive sense of identity is the defining characteristic of one of the greatest football teams of modern times, Barcelona FC (Barça). Reflecting on a recent victory over Real Madrid in one of their famous Clasico games, Lowe wrote,

> '*Barça's coach, Pep Guardiola, praised his side because even when they trailed, even when they doubted, they remained faithful to their philosophy, their identity. They have one. When it comes to the Clasico, Madrid still do not. Maybe that is the greatest difference of all.*'[8]

While history can help to instil a sense of belonging, each team has to forge its own identity. And the nature of this identity must be tailored to the characteristics of that group of people and be made clear and obvious to all. But how can this be achieved? One simple technique is to ask the team and management collectively to come up with a number of short words that define what the team is, and to use these words as a constant reminder through the good times as well as the not so good.

Creating a sense of identity that is real and powerful is not difficult but timing is critical to the enterprise. If a sense of identity comes too soon in a team's development, there may be confusion over what the team is. If it comes too late, the team may have already defined itself in a way that will not necessarily improve or sustain a healthy level of performance.

Another common identity problem encountered with many teams is that the team defines itself not by what it is but by what it *isn't*, or by what it thinks it ought to be. A practical consequence can be that the team will then play *reactively* rather than *proactively*. Put another way, they wait to see how the opposition plays rather than dictating terms and stamping their own mark on the game. In preparation for competition, this tendency may extend to focusing attention exclusively on ways of countering the opposition, instead of playing your own game. Clearly, match preparation must involve both the reactive and the proactive but without a strong and positive sense of identity then there is a danger that play reverts to planning how to avoid defeat instead of how to win, and preparing for failure reaps its due rewards. Interestingly, according to several of his former players, in his team talks Brian Clough, one of England's most successful if enigmatic soccer managers, always attached far greater importance to his own team's play rather than ways of countering the opposition:

> '*I worked, taught, coached, cajoled – call it what you want – all with the aim of getting the most out of my lot because, provided I achieved that, I knew that the opposition would have too much on their plate to surprise us.*'[9]

Building teams – or team building?

For many organisations in sport, as in business, team building has often been seen as essential, but it may be worthwhile reflecting for a while on the pros and cons before going further. History shows that in the wrong hands, team building can do more harm than good unless it is well managed and has deliberate objectives that tally with the identity of the team and with what the team needs to do to achieve success.

Over recent years, many professional sports teams have felt that unless they have been away on the obligatory team-building or bonding holiday before the start of the season then they have missed something out. Why? No one seems to be absolutely sure but since everyone else is doing it, then it has to be right. What can be ignored in the process are the potential costs when teams fell out or where different activities occupy players' minds at the expense of forging a unit that actually plays well together on the pitch and training ground.

As one extreme example, Leicester City's notorious mid-season 'jolly' to Spain in 2004 springs to mind. Eight players were taken in for questioning by Spanish police following allegations of rape by two women. Sadly, this was not the first time the team had hit the headlines for its overseas antics. Four years previously the entire squad had been asked to leave the same Costa del Sol resort because of a well-documented catalogue of unruly and anti-social antics.

To understand why such trips may or may not be useful, we need to return to earlier discussions for a moment. There may be opportunities for 'forming' and 'storming', or getting to know one another as individuals, and also the experience may help to establish a sense of identity. But against these benefits, is the experience likely to achieve longer-term objectives in terms of actually playing together as an effective unit? According to some commentators, team building enhances loyalty to the team and coach, and harnesses support among team members. Granted, such jaunts will allow players to become acquainted, but could this have been achieved just as easily, and at a fraction of the cost, in less exotic locations including the training pitch and the changing room?

Some teams have taken the team-building experience to an entirely different plane by replacing the 'jolly' with another hackneyed and dangerous message, 'No pain, no gain'. Boot camps for teams prior to major tournaments became fashionable in the 1990s but hard evidence to support their benefits is difficult to find. By contrast, the anecdotal evidence cataloguing the harm and hurt that these experiences have delivered is easy to unearth. One of the most notorious of these camps was the one used by the South African rugby union team in their disastrous build-up to the 2003 World Cup. This camp involved a whole series of bizarre challenges that are still the stuff of legend. Unfortunately, the consequence of Kamp Staaldraad was lots of pain but very little gain as the Springboks were eliminated in the quarter finals of the competition after a series of inept performances, followed equally swiftly by the resignation of their coach, Rudolph Straeuli. A short quote from a contemporary commentary on this particular team-building experience is interesting:

'Many rugby observers also pointed out that trying to eliminate all individuality from a team could be counterproductive, as there are many times during a rugby match when individual initiative can make the difference between victory and defeat.'[10]

What makes a good team member?

Looking at the histories of both professional and amateur sport, there is clear evidence to suggest that certain individuals are more at home in individual sports while others perform better in a team environment. For some, the collective drives them to ever greater heights while for others personal mastery and control through individual achievement is what matters most. Even within certain sports, such as bowls, tennis or badminton, some players perform at their best in singles competitions while others shine in the team events. In track athletics and swimming, there have been athletes who only ever revealed their true potential in relays as opposed to individual events. One famous example was the 400m athlete of the 1980s, Phil Brown, who could always be relied on to produce a spectacular time as part of a very successful GB relay team but never came close to matching these achievements in individual events.

Why it is that motivation and performance are influenced in this way is still not clearly understood but almost certainly a number of variables ought to be taken into account. Also, it is worth remembering that performance and motivation are not directly related and so it may be that a team happens to provide the correct motivational environment for those who, without knowing it, find that individual events take them outside their individual zone of optimum functioning (see Chapter 4).

In addition, if an athlete is burdened with either a fear of failure or a fear of being evaluated by others (Chapter 3) then the team provides a safer environment in which to perform. A related psychological construct involves 'diffusion of responsibility', or 'a trouble shared is a trouble halved'. The burden of expectation is reduced dramatically when you are one of many in a team. In a similar way, some players welcome the freedom provided by 'coming in off the bench' as a substitute in a team sport. Again, fear of failure is lowered and inhibitions are reduced.

A second factor to bear in mind is the culture or society that provides the backcloth for the team. One way in which societies are categorised is along the dimension of 'collectivism–individualism'. Certain cultures and societies place a high value on individualism (most obviously the USA) while other countries (most obviously former Eastern bloc countries such as China) value collective action and downplay the significance of individual ambition. From its pioneering infancy to the present day, the USA has placed great store by individual and personal achievement, often portrayed as 'against all odds'. In stark contrast, many Eastern bloc countries valued collectivism and the strength of the group above any one person.

Players from collective cultures may find themselves more at ease and inspired in team events while those from societies that value individualism may struggle with the competing motives of the individual and the collective. Golf's biennial Ryder Cup competition between the USA and Europe provides a fascinating glimpse into such issues, where the American star players often seem ill at ease with the team basis of the competition while many of the European golfers genuinely seem to welcome and thrive in this environment, relishing the experience as refreshing and different from the daily grind of the professional tour.

Those who value collectivism may argue that personal ambition is the eighth deadly sin while collective ambition is one of the noblest of human virtues. This may be an exaggeration but without doubt the inspiration of team success does not burn as deeply in some as in others, and an acknowledgement of this fact can go a long way towards helping establish a motivational climate that will 'work' for a diverse group of players, whatever their sources of motivation, personal or team.

The third question to consider is: what qualities are we looking for in team players? The answer to this question is deceptively easy – individuals. Good teams are not made up of clones or robots who are not allowed to be themselves. Instead, there is a need to strike a very delicate balance – creating an environment that values individuality but one that is bound in a team context where individual goals can still matter yet not as much as the team's. Individual ambition may be important but in a good team it should never be allowed to stand in the way of the collective.

Home and away: Teams in context

The influence of venue on team performance has been subject to close scrutiny, especially the phenomenon of 'home advantage'. Intuitively you would assume that playing at home brings an automatic advantage but research reveals a more complicated picture. In one notable study, the results of several thousand professional games played in the US were analysed to discover if home advantage actually existed.[11] The authors did indeed find some evidence of home advantage in baseball (53 per cent home wins), ice hockey (64 per cent), American football (60 per cent) and basketball (64 per cent), although the authors went on to caution setting too much store by home influence. In fact, they found the effect was most pronounced for teams already riding on a tide of success, with high quality teams appearing to be boosted by home support. In contrast, poorer teams may actually play better away from the scrutiny of home fans. What is more, home advantage often disappears in the latter stages of competitions, unless the team happens to be defending a title.

What is meant by 'home' is also interesting. Home may not actually be home at all but the *perception* of home. For example, one study of a US college basketball team that had to play at five different home venues while its stadium was being rebuilt still revealed home advantage in all five 'home' venues.

Home may be where the fans are, but even this statement must be qualified, because the *nature* of home support is critical. Some supporters are notoriously difficult to please and place such a burden of expectation on their teams that players often welcome an away trip. On the other side of this coin, verbally aggressive home crowds have been shown to have a powerful effect on away teams and can successfully be used to create a fortress mentality, a powerful tactic that has been used by many coaches and managers over the years.

Looking at the play itself, other research would suggest that venue can influence performance in subtler ways and including team discipline. In sports such as soccer, American football and basketball, it has been found that the incidence of reactive aggression, for example fouling or abusing officials, relates positively to the distance from home.

Even the nature and size of the crowd, as well as the design of the stadium, will play its part, with crowd density rather than actual size being critical. The special atmosphere created by certain grounds is legendary in particular sports, and is a factor that must be taken into account when preparing any team. For example, within US college basketball, Duke University is famous for the fervour of its supporters, and the wall of noise and colour that they're able to sustain throughout a home game.

Drawing all this work together it would seem that venue and crowd, home and away, can have a significant effect on performance and results,[12] if they are not well managed. At the same time, from a performance perspective, is it sensible to allow these factors to have an unregulated effect, or would it be more sensible to prepare teams to play wherever they happen to be and to have in place routines that ensure what happens on the pitch is isolated from these factors – while making sure your opposition are still bombarded with the slings and arrows of outrageous fans? The answer is likely to lie in accommodating both issues, using the venue card when it yields benefits (the 'fortress' mentality) but also having techniques for insulating players from these effects when they could interfere (same game, same rules, different venue).

Many hands: Light work or spoiled broth?

So many proverbs refer to the effects of others on our behaviour that it shouldn't come as a surprise to learn that we *do* behave differently in the presence of other people than when we are alone. Two experiments dating from the early 1900s first heralded the significance of these effects in sport. The first compared the times of cyclists who were training either alone, with clubmates or in competition.[13] Norman Triplett found a steady improvement across the three conditions with the poorest times alone and the fastest in competition. In the second study, by Ernst Meumann, the weight that was lifted by men exercising in a training gym when alone was contrasted with the weight they lifted when the author returned to watch them 'pump iron'. Consistently their performance improved when being watched, although they were not conscious of the effect.[14]

'Social facilitation' describes what is happening in both these examples. We work harder in the presence of a team or an audience than when we are alone and especially when we know we are being evaluated. Later research found that the effect was most positive for well-learned, routine tasks but was negative for new or complicated tasks. Which performers are most likely to be adversely affected? No surprises, those who are still learning – novices. In fact, the good become better, the bad become worse, and this was shown dramatically in an experiment carried out in a pool hall some years ago. Players were secretly rated as being above or below average based on their potting accuracy, and then a group casually stood and watched them play. With an audience those players who were above average improved while those who were below average missed even more.[15]

The implications of these studies are considerable. First, it may be better to insulate athletes from evaluation while they are learning new skills. Second, once the routines are well drilled then it is important to simulate match conditions during training, otherwise the crowd may later interfere with effective execution. Third, as a team moves forward in a tournament and the likelihood of performing in front of larger crowds increases, it is important to make sure that preparation for each game takes this into account, for example by stepping-*down* (not stepping-*up*) the build-up to each game.

The second social phenomenon worth mentioning is known as 'social loafing'. The research evidence here is clear. When we are working in a team, and especially when we know that our individual contribution can't be monitored, then subconsciously we take our foot off the gas or accelerator. A very early experiment in France involved measuring the force exerted by up to six people pulling on a rope compared with the same people acting in isolation. Repeatedly, in the team situation individuals only performed at around half what they had shown they were capable of when alone.

Along with personal responsibility, many factors will influence the extent of social loafing including the strength of team identity, the degree of task cohesion, and the extent of trust between team members.[16] Again the implications are considerable. It seems that there should be no hiding place for the individual within the collective, and players must be given feedback on individual as well as team performance to constantly remind them that they are being personally monitored.

Historically, both social facilitation and social loafing have been described separately but over recent years there has been a tendency to describe these team influences in conjunction. In summary, the combined effects are as follows.

Social influences: It all depends!

When the presence of others increases evaluation of a player's performance then easy or well-learned tasks will improve because we are more highly motivated ('social facilitation').

... **but** the execution of more difficult or creative skills may be impaired because of an increase in stress ('social inhibition').

When the presence of others shields us from personal evaluation, performance on easy tasks may become worse because we do not care – especially where goals are not well defined ('social loafing').

... **but** performance on difficult tasks may improve because we are less anxious in a team setting ('social security').

The last word

Over the years a great deal of time and effort has been spent writing about teams but in our view, there is a danger of overcomplicating matters. Teams should be constructed and managed primarily to provide an environment where individual talent can flourish and where the collective can become greater than the sum of its parts. As Phil Jackson, former coach of the Chicago Bulls basketball team (six-times NBA champions) put it:

> 'Good teams become great ones when the members trust each other enough to surrender the "me" for the "we".'[17]

The detritus that collects around teams often muddies the water, making us lose sight of these core principles. But you have to act with these principles in mind if you want to make a difference to a team; or as Cloughie (Brian Clough) once observed:

> 'You don't change a stagnant pool by staring at the water; you have to disturb it – eliminate the pollution and introduce the elements that can make it fresh again.'[18]

While this may sound easy, the person-management skills that must be employed to achieve this goal and to keep a team on track and hungry for success are considerable, and this inevitably brings us to the final stage of our journey: how to create and sustain such an environment. Read on.

9 Leading and managing

What makes a good captain, coach or manager? As you glance back through earlier chapters, you will find that we have already posed similar questions, including 'What makes a champion?', 'What makes the winning mind?' and 'What makes a winning team?'. It will probably come as no surprise to learn that the answer to the first question will be the same as the rest – it all depends! Good leaders in sport, as elsewhere, come in all shapes and sizes, and so searching for a single formula to explain their success is futile.

To illustrate, take any sport and then list who you would rate as the five 'best' managers or captains. Now briefly sketch the psychological profile of each. Almost certainly you will notice that they differ radically from each other not only in their management styles but also their personalities. Admittedly, there may be some who you like or admire more than others – but in terms of success, a consistent winning formula is hard to pin down.

Psychologists have spent a great deal of time trying to define what makes a good leader and reluctantly they have concluded that the search is pointless. Instead, attention has now turned away from a search for personality types and towards the practical functions that leaders must perform, and the circumstances in which they must operate.

As a starting point, we propose that the primary task of good leadership is not to crave fame and glory, boost one's ego or exert power and influence for its own sake. Instead the primary function of a coach or manager is to maximise the potential of those you are privileged to lead. To emphasise this point, consider what the former South African President, Nelson Mandela, had to say about leadership:

> 'It is better to lead from behind and to put others in front, especially when you celebrate victory when nice things occur. You take the front line when there is danger. Then people will appreciate your leadership.'[1]

In the world of sport, some great leaders have loved basking in the spotlight – but some of the greatest have taken their lead from Nelson Mandela. One man who fitted this bill particularly well was the legendary basketball coach John Wooden, who sadly died in June 2010 at the age of 99.

John Wooden

John Wooden was raised on a small farm in Indiana from where he went on to gain a scholarship to Purdue University. A talented and hugely competitive basketball player himself, he became an All-American college player before turning to coaching at the age of 38. In a remarkable career spanning 27 consecutive years with the UCLA Bruins (1948–1975), he succeeded in catapulting the team from the depths of the Pacific College Conference to the pinnacle of their sport, with an unsurpassed record including 88 consecutive victories, 10 NCAA championships (including seven in a row), 38 consecutive NCAA tournament victories and four years where the team went undefeated for the entire season.

The following excerpt, taken from a fan's online tribute, eloquently captures the man – and his many achievements.

> '*Not too keen on flamboyance, Coach Wooden was a modest man who did not seek the limelight; and at the same time, showed the utmost grace and decency to all UCLA's opponents – win or lose. As for his coaching record, neither an 80.6% winning percentage and winning ten NCAA championships define the man completely. Rather, it is the respect he still garners today from those who are in or simply follow college basketball, which define him best. Undoubtedly, John Wooden was the greatest coach ever in any sport, and is the measuring stick for which all other great coaches of all sports will be measured until the end of time.*'[2]

How was John Wooden able to bring out the best in those he coached, year after year? The following quotes from the man himself begin to reveal the basis of his

John Wooden (1910–2010) (Reproduced with kind permission of CoachWooden.com)

success. This approach did not rely on cheap tricks or gimmickry but the promotion of a philosophy that meshes very closely with the principles described throughout *Pure Sport*.[3, 4]

In the words of John Wooden . . .

- Don't let what you cannot do interfere with what you can do.
- If you're not making mistakes, then you're not doing anything.
- Be more concerned with your character than your reputation, because your character is what you really are, while your reputation is merely what others think you are.
- Do not let either praise or criticism affect you. Let it wash off.
- Ability may get you to the top, but it takes character to keep you there.
- Don't measure yourself by what you have accomplished, but what you should have accomplished with your ability.
- In anything, failure to prepare is preparing to fail.
- Be quick, but don't hurry.
- A player who makes a team great is more valuable than a great player.
- Talent is God-given. Be humble. Fame is man-given. Be grateful. Conceit is self-given. Be careful.

Adding value

Measuring leadership solely by the number of trophies on the shelf can be misleading. A far more useful measure is the principle of 'adding value' as captured by the simple question, 'What talent and resources were available and what was achieved?' On both counts, John Wooden was exceptional. In the early years, he was able to build a team with limited resources. Beyond that time, he had the management skills and coaching acumen to be able to keep building and rebuilding the team, in the process creating a sporting dynasty.

John Wooden did enjoy fame in later life but some of the greatest sports coaches or managers will remain unsung local heroes who, against all odds and with minimum resources, create an environment where potential talent is realised and, in team sports, where the team becomes greater than the sum of its parts.

Equally, inspirational captains are often those who achieve great things but with limited resources, or who mould a team during its formative years – sometimes referred to as 'cultural architects'. In truth, the history of sport is littered with examples of those who were later labelled as 'great' captains and coaches but perhaps were nothing more than exceptionally lucky to be linked to a team that had reached its prime – they happened to be in the right place at the right time. This accidental heroism contrasts with truly great captains and coaches who were able to lift and inspire their teams to achieve great things from nowhere and against the odds.

The credibility gap

Time and time again, perversely it would appear that one essential selection criterion for both managers and captains seems to dominate all others – how good the person is, or *was*, as a player. To be frank, a quick scan of the great coaches and managers of all time would suggest that this question is largely irrelevant when it comes to actual performance in a leadership role.

Admittedly, from a practical perspective, when it comes to choosing a captain there is a performance threshold that must be passed before a player can be considered eligible. Put bluntly, can the player expect to hold down a regular place on the team? Beyond this eligibility issue, playing ability alone is not likely to relate to captaincy skills – and may even have a negative influence if other players feel they can hide behind the star performer, or if the burden of responsibility inhibits the player in question.

History shows that many of the greatest captains in sport were not great players but they did bring the team together in a way that added value well beyond their individual playing contribution. With this in mind, for the manager or coach the task of selecting a captain becomes the challenge of finding the person who best captures the values and identity of the team, whether formed or to be formed.

Perhaps this was Clive Woodward's greatest triumph as the manager of England's World Cup winning rugby team back in 2003. He chose Martin Johnson as his captain, a man who personified the rugged, no-nonsense, forward-oriented English style of play at that time. Interestingly, Woodward revealed that he used five criteria in choosing Johnson as England captain.[5] First, he felt that the player had to be the best in his position in the squad. Second, he had to demonstrate the capacity for thinking clearly under competitive pressure. Third, he had to be someone who could command the respect of all his team-mates. Fourth, he had to be 'at one' with the coach in conveying key messages and values to the team. Finally, he had to have some previous experience of the job or have shown leadership skills at a level just below international competition. This last criterion is interesting in light of subsequent events in 2008.

Martin Johnson shone brightly as a player and as a captain, and, on the basis of his fantastic track record, he was thrown headlong into the role of England team manager on 1 July 2008. Sadly for Martin, he had absolutely no previous management experience, and the rest is history – he resigned in November 2011 in the aftermath of a post-mortem on England's poor performance in the 2011 World Cup in New Zealand.

Was Martin Johnson himself to blame? Not at all, he was clearly and rightly honoured to have been offered the post – but those in the Rugby Football Union (RFU) who chose someone with little previous experience of managing at either club or national level must surely shoulder responsibility. In actual fact, given his inexperience, Martin's record as England manager was remarkably good, culminating in the Six Nations triumph in 2011.

This example is not unique by any means, and it is interesting to note that increasing attention within sport psychology is now falling not on individuals in

Martin Johnson (as England manager) (Courtesy of Inpho Photography)

leadership roles but on sport organisations more generally, to scrutinise the ethos and characteristics of sport clubs and governing bodies so as to identify factors linked to success and positive sporting cultures.

Many of the greatest coaches and managers, and even captains, may not have had great talent as players but were still able to bring superb qualities to team management. Take professional soccer. Research[6] has shown that of the 26 managers who coached winning teams in the Premiership (formerly the First Division) in England between 1945 and 2000, fewer than one in five (20 per cent) had ever won more than six international caps. Remarkably, managers including Bob Paisley and Bill Shankly (both of Liverpool) and Sir Alex Ferguson (Manchester United) were never capped by their native country, Scotland. Similarly, Arsène Wenger (Arsenal) never played for France and José Mourinho was never capped for Portugal. Summing it all up, when asked if it was necessary for a great manager to have been a great player, Arrigo Sacchi (who won two European Cups as manager with AC Milan but had never even played professional soccer) joked:

> *'What's the problem here? . . . If you want to be a good jockey, it's not necessary to have been a horse!'*[7]

Admittedly, to understand the game and all its intricacies at the highest level may require some experience and knowledge of that world but to place excessive emphasis on playing experience alone can be dangerous – and expensive.

In conclusion, the question of credibility appears to drive the constant search for those who have achieved as players and yet the significance of this criterion is at best short lived. The past soon becomes forgotten if the square peg doesn't fit the round hole.

Ten steps to sporting leadership

From what we've said so far, it should be clear that good leaders can't simply be pulled off the shelf. At the same time, can we uncover any ingredients that appear to come together in sporting leaders? Having sifted through the literature, we have identified ten qualities that we have found are often associated with successful leadership in sport.

1. It has to matter

Of all the defining qualities of sporting leaders, there is one that cannot be ignored – passion. In other words, it has to matter. Without commitment, a person's capacity to genuinely inspire others will always be questionable. This does not always mean having 'charisma' or great skills of oratory but it *does* have to matter. Some people have taken this quality well beyond the limits, and at such times too much commitment can be as dangerous as too little (see Chapter 2).

The legendary Liverpool Football Club manager Bill Shankly (1913–1981) once famously remarked,

> 'Some people think football is a matter of life and death. I assure you, it's much more serious than that.'

This is a fantastic one-liner but in our heart of hearts we all know that it isn't really true. Nevertheless, Shankly inspired others to greatness because of his personal and unbridled passion for his sport and for Liverpool FC.

This brings us to an important question. When all is said and done, does sport really matter that much? After all, in comparison with many things in life, such as illness and death, it is clearly less important. But strangely, having come to terms with the fact it doesn't *really* matter as much as you first thought then it *can* matter all the more because of that honest acknowledgement of the purity of the endeavour – in other words, pure sport. This sense of perspective is a key theme underpinning *Pure Sport*, and one that we have returned to time and time again: You have to care – but not too much.

Not everyone can or should display the raw, unbridled passion of Bill Shankly. To try to be someone that you are not will take you down an uncomfortable road. Some may prefer the quiet rage while others the ice man, others the extrovert, others the flamboyant showman. There is no magic formula but somewhere within you the flame has to continue to burn brightly and when it doesn't, it may be time to let go.

2. Letting go

Many coaches and managers bring extraordinary levels of commitment to their sport, and then assume that all those they work with must also carry the same passion. Passion matters – but then we encounter a paradox. Good leaders must know *how* and *when* to let go. As Zen masters tell us in the martial arts, to gain control you have to know when to give up control.

In any walk of life involving supervision and the nurturing of skills and knowledge, the true sign of a job well done involves letting go or voluntary redundancy. The gentle hand on the tiller may never disappear completely but for long periods of the voyage the auto-pilot should become just as effective. Knowing that this end point, *empowerment*, is a happy consequence of good leadership should not be forgotten. Too many leaders find letting go of the reins difficult but any well-managed team or athlete must aim to reach a point in their development where the manager, coach or even captain should be prepared to quietly relinquish the driving seat – for stages of the journey at least.

3. Reflecting

As the previous point makes clear, a good leader in sport must have the capacity not only to look *outwards* – to devise tactics, to analyse and assess – but also to look *inwards* – to constantly reflect and adjust his or her own behaviour. Fortunately, many of the performance management skills already described in Chapter 3 are directly transferable to the world of coaching and management.

Performance profiling in particular gives you a way of systematically evaluating your strengths and weaknesses as a coach. Goal setting is also important in providing practical techniques for effecting change. In the spirit of Chapter 3, the profiling attributes you choose have to be personal but as a starting point you could refer to the checklist over the page. This was developed spontaneously during a workshop we ran for top-level coaches across many team and individual sports a few years ago. When asked to define the characteristics of a good coach, these skills and characteristics were identified.

Unless you wear your underpants over your trousers, it is unlikely you could hope to possess all of these qualities – but knowing what you *can't do* as well as what you *can do* then equips you with the knowledge of which gaps need be filled and how to fill them.

In general terms, psychologically we are most comfortable and least challenged when we are surrounded by those who are like us and who reinforce our views. Difference is more challenging than similarity but good teams thrive on the challenge of diversity. With this in mind it is critical to have the courage to use people who complement you rather than simply reflect or reinforce you – in other words, those who fill your gaps rather than reinforce your defences. Many of the most successful management teams in sport have been built on this principle – complementarity yet difference. Or put more bluntly, beware the 'yes' men and women!

Essential coaching qualities

Personal qualities	Interpersonal skills	Technical skills	Knowledge
Energetic	Delegator	Goal setter	Sport-specific
Visionary	Effective manager	Analyst	Tactical awareness
Confident	Networker	Counsellor	Biomechanics
Enthusiastic	Listener	Innovator	Physiology
Honest	Communicator	Planner	Psychology
Resilient	Empathiser	Decision-maker	Nutrition
Punctual		Tactician	Political sense
Positive thinker		Administrator	Medical
Self-disciplined		Selector	Knowing when to walk
Committed			Sceptical enquirer
Patient			
Adaptable			
'Personality'			
Stress manager			
Questioning			

4. Adapting

The late Brian Clough was a soccer legend, and especially when working in concert with his sidekick, Peter Taylor. Between them they plucked first Derby County and then Nottingham Forest from obscurity to the dizzy heights of national and international league and cup success. Euphemistically, their combined management style is perhaps best described as idiosyncratic, being liberally laced with the capacity to surprise – especially in team preparation techniques. In one famous example, before Nottingham Forest's victory over Malmo in the 1979 European Cup, Clough supplied bottles of beer to his players on the bus that took his team to the stadium before the match! This unconventional idea stemmed from a well-founded belief that players perform best in a relaxed frame of mind, or in his words,

> 'Nottingham Forest would be represented by good players who were relaxed . . . That's why we had beer on the coach . . . Forest's footballers weren't uptight footballers when they took to the field.'[8]

Along with Peter Taylor, Clough was able to mould both young players and previously discarded older players into formidable teams with a distinctive style of football. On the strength of his proven achievements, Clough alone was invited to take over from Don Revie at Leeds United.

The Leeds team that Brian Clough inherited was well established and had achieved incredible success over several years. Many of the players were seasoned internationals who did not respond well to Clough's unique and directive style of management. Within 44 days the relationship had ended. As he reflected many years afterwards,

'I was confronted by a seething, resentful, spiteful dressing room when I arrived on my first morning . . . Leeds had done it all . . . They weren't threatened, any of them, because they felt they were bigger than me.'[9]

A salutary lesson for Brian Clough and for any aspiring team manager – new brooms may sweep clean but they can also be broken in the process.

In that era, Clough and Taylor made a superb management team for aspiring clubs – but that management style did not transfer to the bear pit of Leeds United. The capacity to change and adapt is a core principle of good leadership, and it is a dangerous strategy to assume that reputation alone will allow you to impose a style; it may work but it is a high-risk strategy with no guarantee of success.

A more sensible approach may be 'softly softly' – carefully and quietly assessing the situation before deciding how best to proceed. Sometimes this may involve going with the existing flow until sufficient credit has accumulated, sometimes imposing your will earlier if the situation is critical. Whatever else, this must be a careful, considered response as opposed to a hasty gut reaction.

In a similar vein, adapting to the changing needs of the team or athlete is critical in continuing to foster a healthy relationship. Sport is littered with stories of successful coach–athlete relationships that have foundered during the '*sturm und drang*' (storm and strife) of adolescence, or even beyond, for no other reason than the coach has failed to recognise that the athlete is growing up. The relationship, and the coach, must change or perish in the process.

Athletes and players look for different types of support and advice at different stages of their careers.[10] Young athletes generally need considerable social support early on but this need decreases as time goes by. In addition, too much emphasis on skills training can be de-motivating for young people. Technical advice is often most appropriate in mid-career while more mature athletes will often want personal support to help them through the ups and downs of elite competition.

When it comes to leadership and coaching, to be honest there is little point in bombarding you with theory. Both sport and industrial psychology are littered with dozens of leadership theories and models. As previously mentioned, while each may have a different focus and vocabulary, all acknowledge that there is no magic formula for predicting who will be a good leader – and no one style that will be successful across a range of situations.

Instead, sports coaches, managers or captains must develop the ability to assess changing situations and use a style which is in keeping with circumstance, meeting the needs of others and the demands of the situation. In the words of the former British Prime Minister and statesman, Benjamin Disraeli (1804–1881):

'I must follow the people, am I not their leader?'

5. Motivating

'Coaches who can outline plays on a black board are a dime a dozen. The ones who win get inside their players and motivate.'[11]

Vince Lombardi (Courtesy of Inpho Photography)

A good leader must have the capacity to motivate others, But don't imagine that this is a mystical art. It is a *science* that is understandable and the necessary skills are transferable. At the risk of repeating the messages of Chapter 2, it is important to recognise that motivation is not just about a list of factors but is a process, a process that moves us – that gets us out of bed in the morning just as it spurs an athlete to dig deep into dwindling physical reserves at the end of a gruelling competition.

A useful psychological model for describing the process of motivation has already been outlined in Chapter 3.

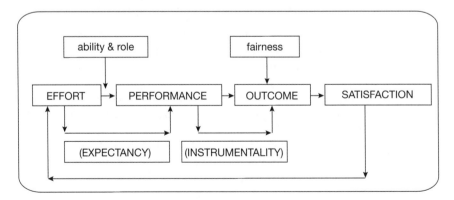

The process of motivation

To be motivated, initially the player must be able to recognise that increasing his or her effort can positively change performance (**Expectancy**), the size of the effect being influenced by ability (perceived and actual) and the role or position that the person is asked to play. Next, **Instrumentality** refers to the player's belief that an improvement in performance will reflect in an increase in rewards. Without this recognition then it is unlikely that greater effort will be expended.

The term **Outcome** does not simply refer to concrete rewards or benefits (e.g., cups, titles, money, status, prestige) but includes intrinsic factors such as a sense of mastery, control, well-being, enjoyment and self-esteem. Too much emphasis on extrinsic rewards can be de-motivating in the longer term while intrinsic motivation provides a more solid foundation for ongoing success. Furthermore, it is not absolute reward but what we receive relative to others – am I getting as much or more or less for what I do?

To apply this model successfully in everyday situations, the first step involves really getting to know what makes each one of your players or athletes tick. Only then is it possible to use this framework for understanding individual problems and delivering effective remedies. Perhaps the player feels that outcomes or rewards do not depend on personal performance, that their place is secure or that they will be dropped whatever they do – in other words, their fate is sealed? Perhaps the player feels undervalued or believes that s/he is not able to improve performance however hard they try? Perhaps the player's personal goals and rewards are no longer the same as those of the team or club, or the outcomes are not clearly defined?

Whatever is the case, by systematically applying this model it is possible to pinpoint where the problem lies and to work out a positive way forward. It gives the coach, captain or manager the opportunity to pinpoint what is going on in each player's head and to understand their priorities, rewards and values – without doubt one of the keystones to successful coaching. As to the practical implications of this model for dealing with players, a number of the most important points are summarised below.

Positive coaching: Five principles

1. Know your players: You must be aware of the priorities, valued rewards and goals of each player in order to maximise potential. No two players will have identical value systems and allowance must be made for differences.
2. Provide positive feedback: Players must be provided with positive feedback on individual performance to maximise effort on future occasions.
3. Relate effort to performance: An individual is only likely to increase effort if there is a belief that this work will actually improve performance. By providing clear feedback on performance, you will improve the effort put into practice.

4.   Relate rewards to performance: A player or athlete must be made aware that a change in performance will lead to either an increase or decrease in outcomes or rewards (either concrete or 'intrinsic') that are valued.
5.   Be challenge oriented: By setting challenging but reachable goals and providing clear feedback on attainment, high levels of performance can be maintained. Goals must not be too distant and must be attainable.

6. Decision making

Moment by moment, successful leadership depends on making the right decisions at the right time. This could include devising and revising game plans, substitutions, training schedules, team selections or longer-term strategies. Ultimately a leader will be judged by the effectiveness of these decisions and so you could assume that decision making is solely about the *quality* of the decisions made. However, this ignores a second crucial element, *acceptance*, or others' willingness to accept and then act on that decision. A good decision means nothing if no one listens and it isn't implemented.

The success of an expedition, as an extreme example, will often hinge on the fine balance between decision quality and decision acceptance, with many disasters precipitated because one or both were not taken into account. On his ill-fated expedition to reach the South Pole, Captain Scott may have inspired his crew to unimaginable heroics by their uncritical acceptance of his decisions, but what about the quality of those decisions? On the other hand, Captain William Bligh may have been one of the greatest navigators and sailors of the eighteenth century but by failing to match the quality of his decisions with acceptance of those decisions by the crew of his ship, *HMS Bounty*, he created a recipe for mutiny. Many leaders are strong in either one or the other but rarely excel in both. An exception to the rule, also from the world of polar expeditions, was the Anglo-Irish adventurer Ernest Shackleton (1874–1922). He was a man who combined extraordinary management skills with sound judgement that ensured not only the success of his expeditions but also the safety and well-being of his crew. One of his greatest attributes was his wry sense of humour, as the advertisement for his 1914–1916 *Endurance* expedition clearly shows:

> '*Men Wanted: For hazardous journey. Small wages, bitter cold, long months of complete darkness, constant danger, safe return doubtful. Honour and recognition in case of success.*'[12]

Successfully balancing decision quality with decision acceptance requires the adoption of a range of management styles, along with knowing which of these styles is best suited to which situation. There may be times when decision quality is critical and you are confident in the information available to you, and so you can take a more directive line. At other times, when both quality and acceptance

Ernest Shackleton (Courtesy of Inpho Photography)

are significant, then you may choose to involve others to some degree, or where acceptance is the overriding concern then delegation may be most successful. Once again, it all depends – and you can depend on the fact that successful managers match the right style with the right situation.

On those occasions where you are compelled to make a high quality decision, other techniques can be brought to bear in order to make sure that a decision is not contaminated by unintentional biases. In some respects this decision-making technique simply builds on and strengthens the thought process that we all use quite naturally when we combine different bits of information in decision making. We accumulate the evidence and then assign different levels of importance to each element before deciding on a course of action. Unfortunately unless this process is systematic there is a real danger that personal biases will creep in and certain elements will assume greater significance than they deserve.

Selecting a hockey player

To illustrate the technique in practice, imagine that you are a hockey coach selecting a team for an important league game. Many players can be pencilled in without much thought. However, there is one key defensive position where you have to decide between two players. Both players have strengths and weaknesses and it will be potentially divisive within the club unless handled sensitively.

To help decide and also to provide you with a solid justification when the team is announced, you first list all the attributes that are relevant to that position in the forthcoming match. Having listed these factors, you then assign a weight to each factor, from 1 (least important) to 10 (most important).

The two players are then scored on each factor, out of ten and their rating is then multiplied by the weight to produce a score that is then totalled and can be compared, as in the table below.

For this particular position, Player A, with a total score of 393, 'gets the nod' over Player B, with a score of 335. Critically, when you now talk to both players you can provide feedback as to why the choice was made and why you believe it was the correct decision. It will also provide the unsuccessful player with feedback that can be translated into positive action for the future. At the end of the day, the

Selecting fairly

Attribute	Weight (W)	PLAYER A		PLAYER B	
		Rating (R)	W × R	Rating (R)	W × R
Speed	7	4	28	6	42
Distribution	6	7	42	6	36
Close stick work	4	5	20	3	12
Passing	3	8	24	7	21
Strength	8	9	72	2	16
Tackling	10	3	30	6	60
'Team member'	5	6	30	4	20
Age	2	8	16	4	8
Fitness	7	7	49	5	35
Competitiveness	8	8	64	8	64
Durability	3	6	18	7	21
TOTAL			**393**		**335**

player may still not like your decision but at least they can clearly understand why you made it.

7. Monitoring

Most of the skills and techniques already described ask the leader to look inwards, to reflect. But introspection must be counterbalanced with an awareness of what is going on *outside*. While the search for personality traits attached to leadership has been disappointing,[13] one attribute that often characterises good leaders is social perception or 'social intelligence' (being aware of others and also having the skills to manage human relations). More generally, leaders typically are described as being either socio-emotionally oriented (primarily concerned with good relations and maintaining harmony) or task oriented (concerned with the task at hand rather than good relations).

Whichever orientation you favour, it is important that the needs, expectations and feelings of others are accommodated in some way and then are reflected in the range of management styles that you use.

Monitoring team dynamics can alert you to emerging issues, including processes of social influence. As an example, although certain individuals may not have been given formal roles or titles in a team or club, they may still be recognised as very influential, and it would be dangerous to ignore the power that these players can wield. Such individuals shouldn't be easily dismissed as disruptive influences and as a threat to authority but instead you should work at how you can harness them to the advantage of the team. This requires person-management skills that may not always sit comfortably with you but the effort will be repaid.

To summarise, three types of awareness should be worked on.

Coaching awareness

Self-awareness: Become aware of your preferred style of coaching/captaincy and try to then expand and develop the range of approaches that you use.

Social awareness: As with motivation, a recognition of the characteristics of the teams and individuals you are working with is important. Also develop the skill of assessing changing situations quickly and adapting your approach accordingly. Try to balance the time that is spent on either technical skills or interpersonal concerns depending on the demands of the situation.

Exchange awareness: Keep in mind that leadership is a two-way process. Followers only allow themselves to be influenced and led if they receive something in return.

8. *Communicating*

Reflecting and monitoring means nothing if the information isn't then communicated effectively. For those new to coaching, management or captaincy there is bound to be some anxiety about giving team talks, etc. As a result, there is a temptation to fall back on a script or the delivery style of someone you admire. This can be reassuring but experience suggests that finding your own style sooner rather than later is likely to be more effective.

Many of the best coaches and captains were far from great orators, preferring to speak with their actions or with a few, well-chosen words. As one example, Roy Keane (who managed Sunderland to Championship success in his first season in charge of the team, 2006–2007) never expected more than ten minutes attention from his players:

> 'There might be a gut feeling, something that came to me during the week about our own team and our own performance. There might be something I might have heard before, but I try to add my own piece to it. We make players aware of the opposition. Five or 10 minutes of the opposition on DVD and then I talk to them. That's all you have really, 10 minutes.'[14]

Traditionally coaches and players alike have placed great store on pre-match talks, supposedly rousing the troops to battle but more likely providing little more than background noise (it is estimated that only around 5 per cent of pre-match talks can be remembered after the game!). Modern changing rooms bear little resemblance to the 'head-banging and hugging' locker rooms of old, with, at long last, an acknowledgement that each player must be given personal responsibility for preparing in a way that works best for them (see Chapter 4).

Equally, half-time tirades have been replaced by more measured use of the available time, often incorporating a 'quiet time' for players to draw breath and reflect before gathering and sharing information and instruction. When reading about great managers there is often a need to take the 'facts' with a hefty pinch of salt. For example, Alex Ferguson's half-time 'hair dryer' treatment has become the stuff of legends. The reality is that this approach is the exception rather than the norm. As he reported back in 2008,

> 'So there are two types of team talk – one if you're doing well and another if you're not. The observations on the first-half are the most important thing. You only have about seven or eight minutes to rectify or resolve the situation if the match isn't going to plan. You should never dodge any issues. I don't know what team talks are like in other dressing-rooms but I try to get to the nub of the problem and solve it as quickly as I can. After that, you have to motivate your players to start the second half. As manager you have to produce the right words and the right volume to make players very aware of their responsibilities and how they can improve.'[15]

In truth it is likely that many of the traditional rants and rituals owe far more to relieving the coach's stress than preparing the players or athletes – and perhaps should be consigned to the waste-bin of history. Also remember that a law of diminishing returns will apply – the first rant may have maximum impact but the second may make less impression, and as for the third, fourth and fifth . . .?

Content over style

Communication works best if you employ a style that is your own. Anyway, it is the *content* of the communication that is much more critical to motivating players and to influencing their performance. Through words and deeds, verbal and nonverbal, the coach and captain have the power to establish the climate for the team, a climate that can either allow players to develop or can inhibit expression and the display of skill. In order to maximise potential, a few simple rules, based on the previous chapters, are worth listing here.

Communicating effectively: Golden rules

Set goals

The highest levels of attainment will be reached where players are aware of what is expected of them, and where the goals that are set are difficult but possible. Describe performance in relation to objective standards or goals wherever feasible. These goals should be short term, difficult but attainable.

Work to an agenda

Have work schedules already to hand before sessions begin but be flexible enough to allow changes should circumstance demand. Communicate your requirements clearly in terms of training schedules, etc.

Provide positive feedback

Let those individuals who reach these goals know that you are pleased. Positive reinforcement works; negative reinforcement is less effective. Use moderation and avoid lengthy comments. Be objective and avoid references to personalities.

Monitor performance

Ensure that players are aware that you are constantly keeping an eye on their performance, in training and during competitions. This does not imply a constant dialogue but subtle reminders of your vigilance.

Emphasise quality

Through monitoring, place the emphasis on quality of work rather than quantity. Again, feedback is important.

Allow honest mistakes

With the emphasis on positive feedback it is important to allow players the freedom to make 'honest mistakes'. Constant criticism is bound to constrain expression and creativity.

9. Being fair

This issue speaks for itself. Sport itself rests on principles of fairness or equity. Without fairness, the activity loses meaning for participants and spectators alike. Equally, it is impossible to continue to motivate and lead in an environment where fairness does not reside as a core value – lose fairness and trust will not be far behind. Ongoing hot debates around, for example, drug abuse in various sports,[16] refereeing decisions and racism in soccer, starkly reveal the central role that fairness plays in sport – and the strong emotions that are stirred when it is felt that unfairness is abroad.

The former England soccer captain, John Terry, found himself at the centre of a storm of controversy over alleged racist comments made to another player, Anton Ferdinand, during a game between Chelsea and Queens Park Rangers in October 2011.[17] In particular his future role as England captain was thrown into question. Could he continue to command the respect of England players, both black and white, with the suspicion that his sense of fairness may be questionable? His decision to retire from international football came not long afterwards.

From a management perspective, one technique to ensure that fairness is sustained is to remain always conscious of what is known as the *principle of social exchange*. All social relationships can be thought of as exchanges, we give and we receive, and we continue to invest in a relationship so long as we feel that we have had a return on our investment. What each person defines as a reward or a cost is unique but it is rare to find a healthy relationship where all parties don't feel they have benefited – in other words, the rewards outweigh the costs. Over long-term relationships, awareness of social exchange ('What did I give, what did I get') becomes less pronounced but in new relationships or when relationships have been damaged, then exchange awareness is heightened ('Look what I did for them, look what they did/didn't do in return'). In these situations it is imperative that there is sensitivity towards feelings of being treated unfairly when interacting with team members or athletes.

Taking this approach further, leadership itself can be characterised as a process of exchange. Leaders are given status and power but in return those who are led will expect to be rewarded, with fair treatment and with success. Once more, in the early stages of a relationship there is heightened awareness of costs and benefits, and it is dangerous to make an assumption that all is hunky dory without relying on regular feedback to check your perception against others.

10. Managing conflict

As Chapter 8 makes clear, in the context of team dynamics, conflict is not a dirty word and healthy conflict or competition is a necessary ingredient in the make-up of any successful team. In turn, this means that a good leader must expect to be a good conflict manager, recognising the positive and the negative sides of conflict before responding in a way that meets the demands of the situation. Before jumping in with both feet, it is worthwhile spending time reflecting on the nature of the conflict and deciding how to respond. When dealing with a conflict, either brewing or brewed, the following questions may help you come to grips with the issues more effectively.

1. Is the conflict genuine or false?

Is this a genuine disagreement between two or more people or is the conflict nothing more than a misunderstanding or communication breakdown. If it is the latter, then the fix is usually more straightforward and involves correcting mis-perceptions and bridging the communication gap before things go from bad to worse. However, if the breakdown in communication is merely symptomatic of a wider problem within the team then this must be addressed at source.

2. Is the conflict positive or negative?

Many conflicts within teams or between coaches and athletes are positive, reflecting genuine differences of opinion, and these should be acknowledged and worked through. Unfortunately unless sorted quickly there is the potential for spillage into other issues, and relationships can become damaged. At the same time, many positive conflicts may not need to be managed at all but actively encouraged if they create a climate that is productive and successful. Deciding the nature of the conflict, positive or negative, will help determine the nature of the intervention, if any.

3. Who is involved?

Determining who the key players are is always important. For example, a major dispute within a club may have been sparked by a disagreement between two players but others then become caught up, sometimes against their will. These innocent bystanders soon find there is no fence to sit on but are asked to take sides. Determining who are the main protagonists and who are the support artists is essential.

4. What are the issues?

Often the history of the conflict will reveal an interesting sequence of events involving the interplay between many factors and including the following sources of conflict.

Sources of conflict

Interests (what I want, what you want)
Understanding (what I understand, what you understand)
Values (what is important to me, what is important to you)
Styles (the way I do things, the way you do things)
Opinions (what I think, what you think)
Identities (who I am, who you are)

Over time, the root cause of the conflict may have been lost or clouded by later events. Unpicking the conflict and its history can be helpful in sequencing resolution techniques. Often this involves dealing with the easiest issues first before moving on to tackle the major bones of contention. Ordinarily, only one of the factors outlined above presents itself as a major obstacle to resolution – and that is *values*. Where one or more players subscribe to a set of values that are out of kilter with the team or club then drastic measures may be called for to remedy the problem. If the conflict is based on any of the others, then the solution is often easier to reach through a managed process of reconciliation.

5. Who is best placed to deal with this and how?

Having taken time to work through the essential elements, the last stage involves coming up with a strategy for conflict resolution based on one or more conflict management styles (see p. 162). It may be that you decide to allow the situation to continue, perhaps if the temperature is still not high enough to guarantee engagement, or you may decide that it is better dealt with by others. Whatever decision you reach it must be a strategic one, not influenced by emotion, in order to increase the likelihood of success.

Conflict management styles

Having thought through the issues, you are now in a position to apply the conflict management style that is best suited to deal with this situation. The literature tends to agree that up to five styles can be used individually or in combination and these are outlined briefly below. Common sense will often dictate which style to employ but even recognising that there are alternatives is helpful, and also acknowledging that we each tend naturally to use one style more often than others. If you are interested in finding out which styles you tend to use most often then try the following web link:

http://www.kilmanndiagnostics.com/catalog/thomas-kilmann-conflict-mode-instrument

Conflict management styles

Forcing (competing)

When to use: Whenever quick, decisive action is vital and especially on important issues where unpopular courses of action need to be implemented fast – e.g., enforcing unpopular rules, discipline, health and safety. It is also a useful style to use on vital issues when you know you are right. Finally, bullies often need to be bullied, otherwise they may try to abuse power or take advantage of you.

Confronting (collaborating)

When to use: This style helps find an integration solution when both sets of concerns are too important to be compromised or when your goal is to learn. It is also useful for merging insights, thereby gaining commitment by incorporating inputs into a joint decision. If hard feelings have been disturbed in a relationship then this style will help to rebuild bridges.

Sharing (compromising)

When to use: Compromising will work best when goals are not too important or worth the effort or potential disruption of more assertive modes. In particular this is true when two opponents with equal power are strongly committed to mutually exclusive goals. The style will help achieve temporary settlements to complex issues under time pressure or as a fall-back when collaboration or competition fails to be successful.

Withdrawing (avoiding)

When to use: When an issue is trivial, of only passing importance, or when other more important issues are pressing. Equally, when you perceive no chance of satisfying your concerns or the potential damage of confronting outweighs the benefits of its resolution. It helps buy time either when emotions are running high, allowing perspective and composure to be regained, or when the gathering of more information outweighs the advantages of an immediate solution. Finally, there may be situations where others can resolve the conflict more effectively or when the issue seems tangential or symptomatic of another more basic issue.

Smoothing (accommodating)

When to use: Accommodate when you realise privately that you are wrong – it will allow a better position to be heard and will show that you are reasonable. It is especially valuable when the issue is much more important to the other person than to yourself. By giving ground you can build up 'social credits' for later issues which are important to you ('you owe me one') and especially when you make clear that you have made a tactical decision to adopt this approach. Accommodating preserves harmony in difficult times and, longer term, it aids the development of subordinates by allowing them to learn from their own mistakes – letting go.

Common sense, aided by structured decision making, can normally succeed in turning difficult situations around. As a manager or coach, on a daily basis, you will already be dealing with conflict, and often very effectively. This guidance may simply reinforce your existing good practices or it may help prevent a drama turning into a crisis.

The last word

In sport as elsewhere, a great deal has been written about what makes a great leader. Reflecting on this literature, it is too easy to stand in awe of those who have been there and done it all, and to feel humbled and inadequate by comparison. Yes, there have been exceptional leaders with remarkable skills throughout the history of sport but equally it is amazing how unremarkable these 'giants' can be when you actually meet them in the flesh! The most striking characteristic they share is that they are comfortable with who they are, they know what they want and they know how to go about getting it. Beyond this, sometimes they have just been fortunate to be in the right place at the right time.

Rather than placing these individuals on a pedestal, our intention has been to learn from previous triumphs and failures alike, and then to show you in very practical ways the factors you can combine to help you carve out your own unique career in sport management. The rest is up to you.

10 The end?

Pure Sport tries to present a practical guide to the world of applied sport psychology. However, this journey is fundamentally different from many others that you may have taken for one simple reason – it should never end.

Why? Two reasons spring to mind. First, until now you've largely been a passenger as we have tried to steer you through the landscape of sport psychology. From now on, things should start to change as you take hold of the wheel and so your personal journey really begins.

The second reason why this chapter does not signal an end is that skill development is not passive and linear but is an active *cyclical* process of constant reflection and renewal. In other words, you have to *keep making it happen* – not waiting for it to happen to you.

Probably the greatest national hunt jockey of all time, Tony McCoy, continues to amaze the racing world by his insatiable hunger for more winners. Graciously receiving accolades, but not allowing them to stand in his way, Tony provides the simple key as to how he is able to keep renewing and re-energising himself:

> *'I found it hard to accept that all the tributes were about me, but back came that old chestnut about me burning myself out and the possibility of snapping mentally and physically. I know it was well meant, but I also know that I've got the best job in the world and the easiest lifestyle – because it's the one I choose.'*[1]

In other words, he enjoys what he is doing and he is choosing to continue doing what he does best, ride horses. It's that simple.

Take another example from the world of motor racing. Sebastian Vettel, who, at 25 years of age, became the youngest ever three-times Formula One World Champion in November 2012, is very clear about what keeps him coming back for more. It is not the prestige, the glamour or the money, it is his undiluted passion for racing.

> *'You need passion to succeed. Yes, being a racing driver is a special job but, generally, if you don't like what you do then you're not going to be very good. You will face a point inside you where you think: "Is this the right thing? Why am I doing this?" . . . Money can be a motivation but it will never make you happy.'*[2]

Sebastian Vettel (Courtesy of Inpho Photography)

A related lesson from sport is worth repeating at this point. If you want it all to be over, the final whistle, or if you mindlessly play down the clock, then you immediately run the risk of undoing all your previous good work. As an old saying goes, don't count the time – make the time count! Also, remember an earlier message – when the going gets tough, the tough keep doing what got them there in the first place.

So, where does that leave you now? Well, as a reminder, let's return to where we began with *Pure Sport*. Put simply, the voyage of exploration that we have tried to chart has one goal in mind – to help you realise your physical potential. If you feel that you have come to the end of that journey and you have nothing left to discover, then we've failed. But so long as you stay actively involved with sport, in whatever role, this journey should never end but should keep driving you onwards and upwards.

Across all sports, there have been many examples of those who failed to test their true potential because they mistakenly felt that they had already reached the end of the road, maybe having achieved a significant goal. Instead they should have paused, celebrated and then duly acknowledged that it was no more than one more stop along the way. On any journey, there will be times when you may choose to rest and admire the view but eventually the need to travel on should stir you to stand up and move on. Without that desire or hunger to journey and see what lies ahead, you are settling for a comfortable life rather than a challenging one –

and you should contemplate putting your feet up. Or in the words of soccer manager supreme, Alex Ferguson,

> 'The past is never enough. A victory only lasts a moment. It's where the next one is that matters.'[3]

Flick back through the pages of *Pure Sport* and you'll see that *nowhere* do we signal an end point but a whole series of new beginnings including all the techniques and skills that you continue to develop and carry with you on your sporting travels. To paraphrase the great writer and traveller, Robert Louis Stevenson, it is the *journey* not the destination that really matters or in his own words,[4]

> 'Little do ye know your own blessedness; to travel hopefully is a better thing than to arrive and the true success is to labour.'

Speaking of a journey, along the way you know that you will meet with good times and with bad times, and both should matter to you – but neither too much. After all, without the one (failure), you can never really enjoy the other (success) (see Chapter 7). What is more, if you are willing to learn, you will continue to learn far more from your disasters than from your triumphs. In the words of Rudyard Kipling's poem 'If', you should strive to learn to, 'Treat those two imposters just the same'.[5]

To make your sporting journey as enjoyable as possible, you must travel light. Experienced travellers know that they move most easily and quickly with the least amount of baggage. Let's face it, if you are carrying someone else's luggage and heading for a destination that was not your choice in the first place, the journey can become tedious and pointless. As a quick reminder, bring to mind these two questions from Chapter 2 – why are you doing it? (Chiefly for enjoyment.) and who are you doing it for? (Chiefly yourself.) These questions provide the simple foundations on which to build and sustain a successful sporting career.

Your kit bag

Travelling light is critical but there are two small pieces of equipment that you may need to have with you on your adventure. The first is a mirror (see Chapter 3). This is not to admire yourself or to check who is coming up behind. Instead, you must use it as a constant way of reminding yourself who you are and where you are. Lose sight of a realistic and honest sense of self-identity and trouble lies around the corner

The second piece of equipment can be hidden well from view. Although it weighs very little, it will keep you moving ahead (see Chapter 2). It is 'the chip', or to be more precise, a chip on the shoulder. Don't regard this as a character flaw or mistakenly confuse it with arrogance or over-confidence. The chip is a positive indication that whatever has been achieved is never enough, and this inner drive continues to fuel the hunger for more. Those who succeed in sport are never quite content, or as Mark Cavendish, one of the most fiercely competitive and successful sprint cyclists of all time, said during an interview at the end of his incredible 2011 season, 'I still want more'. To him, the challenge itself remains his inspiration and driving force,

> *'I never think it's going to be difficult, with me there is no thought of emotion, no thought that it might not be possible . . . The only consequence of anything is going to be crossing the finish line first.'*[6]

What is more, that drive or hunger should never be used as an excuse for sulking when the best laid plans fall apart. Reality can deliver cruel blows but knowing the chip is still fixed on your shoulder is a sure sign that your journey has not come to an end but that you are willing to pick yourself up and move on, learning as you go.

The crude maxim that we offer in Chapter 3 ('Feck it, Do it, Think about it') captures the mindset of someone who is able to go out and perform unburdened by doubt, who keeps analysis in its place but is always willing to learn before moving on, older and wiser. In this way, the journey itself becomes inspiring, with you firmly in charge.

Skills such as those attached to goal setting and profiling (Chapter 3) are critical in helping you stay on track, and equipping you with systematic ways of continuing to review and move forward. These can then dovetail with many of the techniques that we have outlined in Chapters 4, 5, 6 and 7. These techniques must be tailored to your own needs but should provide you with a personal collection of tools that can help you to continue to explore your sporting potential.

To this point, the journey we have described is a solitary expedition, a journey of self-discovery and self-fulfilment. Not surprisingly this is only one part of the equation because sport invariably involves teams, and it is at this point that a heavy qualification must be added to our commentary.

There have been many great and talented athletes who never really understood the team element of their sport for one simple reason – individual desire stood in the way of collective ambition. Everything we have described so far in terms of personal development can continue to flourish in a team environment but only if the individual is willing to buy unreservedly into a critical team value – *collective ambition*. In the words of John Wooden, one of the greatest coaches of all time, when describing the basketball player Lewis Alcindor (later Kareem Abdul-Jabbar), the NBA's highest-ever points scorer with 38,387 across his professional career:

> *'Lewis believed the team came first . . . A great player who is not a team player is not a great player. Lewis Alcindor was a great team player. Why? Because his first priority was the success of the team, even at the expense of his own statistics.'*[7]

This idea of collective ambition is echoed by the 'special one', soccer manager José Mourinho:

Kareem Abdul-Jabbar (Courtesy of Inpho Photography)

> *'Everything is aimed at one thing – the quest for performance. The aim of my form of relationship is not that the players like me, the only objective is the performance of the group. I sacrifice the individual for the collective.'*[8]

Collective ambition may seem rather abstract but it is not a difficult concept to grasp. In fact, we hope that all the messages in *Pure Sport* are neither hard to understand nor difficult to put into practice. To repeat ourselves, sport psychology may not be rocket science but without a bit of solid technical guidance it can be difficult to bring together all the elements that make up 'repeatable good performance' (RGP) in a systematic way.

In our experience, many sportspeople and coaches can be too selective or reactive, cherry picking elements that seem most relevant at that particular moment. In its worst form, this approach involves throwing in a sport psychologist to address a team at a time of crisis – usually just before an important competition. Not surprisingly, these tactics are rarely effective for at least three reasons. For a start they convey a message to players that psychological preparation is not really their responsibility but is best left to an 'expert' outsider. This problem is especially likely to occur at elite-level sport where players often have so much specialist assistance available to them that they can unwittingly become helpless and indecisive. Second, calling in a sport psychologist at the last minute suggests that proper mental preparation is a quick fix rather than a systematic philosophy. Finally, in our experience, any short-term benefits that may be gained from hearing a fresh voice prior to a big match are likely to disappear quickly unless players are persuaded to buy into the entire package.

And that package is precisely what we have tried to explore in this book. Put simply, we hope that *Pure Sport* has shown you how to identify and assemble the mental elements of sporting excellence. Piece by piece, we have hoped to reveal the jigsaw that is commonly known as sport psychology but which actually encompasses the bringing together of thoughts, feelings and actions in the creation of high-quality and consistent sporting performance.

Problems and solutions

Over the years, we have been called on by many people involved in sport to help deal with difficult situations involving both individual athletes and the management of teams. To end *Pure Sport*, we thought it might be useful to sketch some of these problems – and possible solutions.

In each case, we present a question that we're often asked and then outline practical issues that it raises. In keeping with the tone of this book, our advice comes with a health warning. No two people or situations will ever be identical, and so there is very little likelihood that one analysis or intervention will achieve magical results when practised on different people and in different situations. Instead weigh up the facts of each situation and act accordingly. In other words, horses for courses.

In passing, there is an unfortunate trend in popular books on sport psychology to endorse a 'one size fits all' approach where the same psychological strategies (e.g., concentration techniques) are recommended uncritically for a variety of problems and situations. In our experience, strategies must be carefully tailored to individual needs – bearing in mind such factors as the structure of the sport (e.g., whether it is timed or untimed, whether play is continuous or 'stop-start') and athletes' own informal theories about when and how they perform at their best. For example, if you're a golfer, the type and timing of trigger words you use to help concentrate will differ from those you would use in soccer. And whether or not you use any concentration technique *at all* depends on the importance that you attach to mental preparation in the first place, or whether you need them.

Individual performance: Problems and solutions

'I've lost confidence'

From our experience, saying that you've lost your confidence is often a catch-all for lots of underlying issues that reveal themselves in underperformance. In fact, it is probably the most common problem that sport psychologists are asked to deal with. In practice, the statement 'I've lost confidence' usually opens up wider discussion of many issues where the mind has started to impose itself unduly over action, and then performance has suffered. For example, if things have not been going well for you then you may start over-analysing and in the process, digging an even deeper hole (i.e., paralysis by analysis).

At one level, 'confidence' is easy to define. Put simply, it's the *belief* that you can play a certain shot or achieve a certain goal – no matter what. Confident players think they can do it – no matter what. But at a deeper level, confidence is complex. Like any belief, it is shaped by circumstances and so can change. For example, few people are equally confident across all skills. If you're a golfer, you may be more confident with your driver than your wedge. Or if you're a baseliner in tennis, you're likely to be more confident at the back of the court than at the net. Clearly, the fact that confidence is specific to a skill and a situation means that to improve it then you have to *deliberately* work harder on aspects of your game that you least enjoy or want to think about.

A perceived lack of confidence can be the end-product of a process that involves many issues we have spotlighted throughout *Pure Sport*, for example measuring your performance solely by results (see Chapter 3). So you should never fall into the trap of seeing a lack of form as a confidence issue set apart from everything else. Instead, try to develop a more objective and scientific evaluation of your performance to identify the reasons why your form has dipped. This habit of disciplined reflection will help you go back to basics, to identify strengths as well as weaknesses and then use this foundation to develop a programme of rehabilitation, and so gradually re-establish your form.

Speaking of strengths, you may need to remind yourself of your special skills or 'weapons' from time to time, and especially if you have a tendency to judge yourself harshly. These skills are usually ones that you enjoy performing and are most confident about – and they establish a solid platform for the rest of your game.

And remember, you aren't as good as your last game but you *are* potentially *at least* as good as your best ever game. Talent never goes away – but it *can* be mislaid. If your form seems to have slipped, try not to burden yourself with high expectations of making amends by a flawless performance but instead set more realistic goals within a reasonable and attainable timescale. For example, if you're a tennis player whose confidence has dropped because you haven't won for a while, it might be helpful to set yourself a short-term performance target in your next game, such as percentage of first serves.

Also remember that too much confidence can be as dangerous as too little. There may be times when everything comes together but a more realistic expectation is 'repeatable good performance' (RGP), adjusting the bar as you progress. Successfully balancing the three Cs (confidence, commitment and control), and learning to enjoy the *challenges* of competition will provide a much more solid foundation for success than overblown confidence, best summed up not as a 'will win' mentality but '*can* win'.

'*I can't seem to rise to the big occasion*'

This problem may not be as simple as you first think. Perversely, in these circum-stances it is often not the case that the individual is unmotivated but that he or she can't deal with the pressure of the big occasion. That is, the individual actually may be rising too high to the occasion and as a consequence is moving well outside the performance zone that normally works well for them – in other words, you are too stressed. At this point, an old maxim in sport is relevant: Success comes in *cans* not *can'ts*! Managing your anxiety (see Chapter 4) may help to re-establish the critical point on the 'stressometer' that you need to be at in order to play at your best.

If you do find it difficult to rise to the occasion, it may be helpful to look at specific times in the past when you played to your full potential. Remember that if you did it before, you can do it again. By reflecting on what it felt like to be playing at that level, and by reminding yourself of how you prepared for your best performance, you can develop a pre-match routine that you can follow every time you compete. According to many commentators, when in his prime, one remarkable feature of Tiger Woods' preparation for major tournaments was just how unremarkable it was. He knew what worked and so didn't change his routines. In other words, why change a winning formula?

> 'One of the biggest mistakes any player can make is treating the majors as something special. In terms of preparation, Tiger Woods does not do that. Tiger gets a lot of credit for being able to get his game in its best shape for the biggest four weeks of the season, but the fact is that he warms up for every event as if it is a major. That is his "secret".'[1]

For some people, this 'winning formula' may involve learning not to think too much about things outside their control such as the result of the match or how opponents will play. What might help you to block out such negative thoughts are deliberate distractions (e.g., music, other activities) and planned 'time-outs'. Interestingly, many golfers hold conversations with their caddies as they walk between shots simply to prevent themselves from thinking negatively.

Alternatively, it sometimes happens that big occasions bring to mind another problem – the 'what ifs' or fear of failure. If you are worried about letting others down and are focused on the *result* rather than performance then you need to switch your focus to specific, personal performance goals (e.g., 'I'm going to keep up with play' or 'I'm going to follow the player I'm marking no matter where he goes'). Before competition, make sure that you create space to do your own thing and don't be caught up in other people's preparation routines – they may work for them but you know, deep down, that they don't work for you. At the same time, if you are spending too much time analysing and reflecting and this is causing anxiety then deliberately see how you can turn off the spotlight, for example, by actively attending to other matters or by supporting others.

'I can't raise my game for anything other than the big occasion'

Sometimes, those who have 'been there and done that' may start to become complacent and lose the capacity to raise their game for anything other than the biggest stage. If this problem has ever applied to you, then one way of sharpening your 'edge' is to learn to shift your focus away from outcome or results and towards personal performance targets. For example, if you're a footballer who's played hundreds of matches, it's difficult to sustain the work rate that you showed in your first game – unless you give yourself a 'personal best' challenge. Put simply, this means trying your best to work harder and be more active in aspects of your game today than you did yesterday. For example, can you win more tackles in your next game than you did in your last one?

Explicit performance objectives expressed in activity levels are very useful in these circumstances because they remind us of our personal contract. Alternatively, you may need to shift focus from internal to external, and so become more involved in the management and general well-being of other team-mates. This should have a positive effect on motivation and commitment, especially in situations where players have developed the habit of being critical of less experienced team-mates.

'My head isn't right . . . I seem to drift in and out of games'

Younger players, in particular, often complain that they find it difficult to stay focused for the full game. As we explained in Chapter 5, this problem is perfectly normal as our brains evolved *not* to pay attention to any one thing for very long. Chapter 5 also contains many practical techniques that can help you to break your playing time down into more manageable chunks through 'restructuring', to focus on one thought or action, and to switch your concentration from one target to another as required. Interestingly, many top coaches and captains use pre-match or half-time talks to emphasise various stages in a game and to set specific targets that break the whole into smaller parts. Even knowing that you are not required to maintain a single type of 'focus' (e.g., narrow, external) for the entire competition can help you to overcome the problem. After all, forewarned is forearmed.

'I can never reproduce in games what I have shown I'm capable of in practice'

This is a common problem among those who have not developed standard pre-match routines to ensure consistency of approach, or who have not come to terms with the stress levels that work well for them (Chapter 4). Less commonly, this may be because the athlete has lost interest in competition for some reason; where this is the case then it would be important to understand why (see Chapter 3).

For those who can't translate practice into competition, the starting point must be quantifying or measuring how large the gap is before looking at ways of bridging the gap. It is unlikely this will be achieved overnight but instead will involve a measured process that involves minimising the difference between the two, for example by treating competition as no more than another practice session, or making each practice more like actual competition. This problem may take time and effort to resolve but is not insurmountable.

'I often seem to pick up injuries coming up to big games'

It is very common for many sportspeople to report picking up niggling injuries in the build up to important games. Sometimes this trend is merely a by-product of increased vigilance and monitoring and a heightened sense of self-awareness that comes from wanting to ensure that everything is 'just right' for the big day. It's a bit like checking that every door and window of your house is locked before you go on holidays. In itself, this anxiety should not be a major cause for concern and especially where the player has performed well under similar circumstances in the past. On other occasions, reports of an injury may act as a psychological insurance policy or ready-made excuse that can be pulled out of the drawer if performance turns out to be below par – a phenomenon known as 'self-handicapping'.[2] The idea that 'I didn't play well because I had an injury' contrasts sharply with the 'no excuses' mantra of *Pure Sport*.

A related problem may occur if an athlete's fear of failure creates a mindset where s/he doesn't really want to meet the challenge and so uses the injury as an excuse for crying-off ('blobbing out'). This problem may call for a more significant intervention to change the player's orientation to competition from 'I'll die if I lose' to 'I'll do my best to win'. Where the injuries are stress-related, there may be greater cause for concern. For example, an athlete may constantly over-train to compensate for a lack of confidence, and injuries may emerge as a consequence of this excessive regime. Recognising that the problem is there in the first place goes a long way towards fixing it.

'I never play well when ***** is watching; I'll never be as good as *****'

These statements are related and often suggest that the individual has placed too great an emphasis on *external* reference points when judging his or her own performance. The expressions indicate thinking that is burdened by a high fear of failure. The solution is straightforward but can take time – to make the athlete more self-contained and self-evaluative. For example, if someone is constantly looking for ego-stroking by others then deliberately put in place performance evaluation procedures that he or she must complete immediately after competition (see Chapter 3). In this way, the individual will eventually come to rely more on personal judgements than those of others. At the same time, he or she will develop a stronger and more comfortable sense of self-identity, and reference to role models should become less important. This can often be a problem during adolescence, at a time when the person may be looking for reassurance from 'significant' others. And the answer is easy – make them less significant!

'I spend a lot time thinking about the game beforehand, usually "what if" . . .'

As we mentioned earlier, for many competitors too much 'focus' before a game can be just as dangerous as too little. If this problem seems familiar then you should reflect on what worked for you in the past and use this formula to capture medium and short-term pre-competition schedules that create the right mindset for you to play well. Do you need an angry head, to feel chilled, to be distracted, to feel you have been treated unfairly, not respected, top dog, underdog, the list goes on. Whatever state works for you, it is not necessarily one you are comfortable with but the one that has been usually attached to your better performances. For example, if you play best when you don't think about performance then this may involve keeping busy with other things and so restricting head time.

What is more, when thinking about competition it is important to follow one of the golden rules of imagery as outlined in Chapter 6 – always use imagery in a constructive way by visualising positive targets and successful actions. Time spent in mental practice should be deliberate, structured and planned using whatever techniques are appropriate for your sport and for you. After all, why hurt yourself by imagining things going wrong – what is the point? Just lying and thinking about the game is often a recipe for disaster, and filling time more productively, maybe with activities completely divorced from your sport, can often overcome this problem.

'I can't get to sleep before a game'

This is a common problem that is often made worse before competition because we try so hard to have a good night's sleep – for example, we go to bed earlier than usual and in the process disrupt our normal sleep patterns. The result – we end up tossing and turning and simply can't shut down.

The first rule for getting to sleep is don't break with routine. Before competition, always go to bed at the usual time and not too early. Second, try this simple way for drifting off, known as 'chaining'. You have to concentrate hard on this technique but with practice it can be very effective in a matter of minutes. The trick is to simply allow your mind to drift effortlessly from one thought or image to the next without ever questioning why or reflecting where the chain is going. It can be random, it can be circular but never question just allow your mind to drift, until you will find you drift into sleep. Another useful technique to break vicious cycles of thought is to think back over your day, never stopping to evaluate events but simply ordering what happened and when, in minute detail. Again, once the chain of thought that held your attention is broken, sleep can quickly follow. If all else fails, don't lie there and worry, get up, have a hot drink, and go back to bed when you feel ready.

'I'm finding it hard to come back from injury'

This is a familiar issue for many athletes, and especially when the injury is sudden or interrupts a run of good form. The outstanding Irish rugby player Paul O'Connell returned from the British Lions rugby tour to New Zealand in 2005 knowing that he faced surgery and a period of enforced rest. He also had the honesty to recognise that he hadn't played to his potential on tour. His solution was simple. He determined that he would return from injury not just as good as when he left but even better. This is a good example of the type of 'personal best' approach that motivates winners in sport (see also under 'I can't seem to rise to the occasion'). As with Roy Keane (see Chapter 2), he then decided to use the enforced 'time out' to consider how he could improve as a player, and left no stone unturned in the process. So instead of the injury time being a frustrating enforced absence from the game, he structured it with a goal in mind – to come back even stronger, which he did.

In contact sports, awareness of an injury can inhibit play. To overcome this heightened monitoring and state of awareness, it can be helpful to concentrate attention on highly structured short-term performance goals. In this way, one's attention is diverted from the dominant thought, 'How does it feel?' to the more helpful question, 'How did I play?' By way of example, a previous shoulder injury in rugby may dominate thoughts going into a game and especially around tackling. Replace these general anxieties with very focused performance targets, even down to the mechanics of the tackle itself and including body position and contact area.

'If my first touch goes well, that's a great sign but if it doesn't, forget it!'

Fortune telling is bad news for athletes. The above statement is a prime example of someone who admits being out of control and believes that luck, chance or fate is controlling his or her performance. On good days, if things start well then this can inspire confidence, but on bad days the chances of turning a situation around are slim. This type of player will spend the early minutes of a game testing whether or not things are right, and may try to make amends by 'upping the ante' each time to remedy earlier errors. The lack of perceived control in such circumstances is disconcerting, and the chances of making amends diminish over time.

If this problem applies to you, a good solution is to put yourself centre-stage and to highlight the degree of control that you have over your own performance. In particular, in the early stages of competition it is important not to emphasise the first touch but general work rate and activity (e.g., use 'buzz' as your buzz word!), and never to look backwards. Also, remember that the only people who don't make mistakes are people who never try anything at all (see Chapter 7).

'If I make a mistake or if something goes wrong for me I can't get it out of my head'

So many of the issues we have already discussed can reveal themselves in a situation where the spontaneous becomes thoughtful, where thought interferes with action, and especially where past mistakes continue to cast a shadow over present performance. Staying in the here-and-now is critical to good performance (see Chapter 5). Look ahead and you lose sight of what you are doing, look behind and you will find that mistakes and 'what ifs' will cloud your judgement. With practice, there are many mental skills that can be learned to help you 'draw the line' – to consign to history previous mistakes and instead to play it as it comes. We showed you in Chapter 7 how to put your setbacks and mistakes behind you so that you can simply 'get on with it'. In our view, this is mental toughness in action. A good coach will not choose to burden players with history but will have effective ways of clearing away the detritus to allow freedom of expression, to make history. One very practical technique for reminding yourself to draw the line is to do just that, draw a thick black line on the back of your hand as a constant reminder to stay in the present.

'Show me the money!'

As Chapter 2 reveals, the tangible rewards attaching to modern sport can often interfere with performance in many unusual ways. At some stage of a career it is often important to stand back, reassess and remind yourself the reason why you play sport in the first place. If enjoyment has moved into second place behind the trappings that go with success then trouble lies ahead, a lesson that the greatest darts player of all time, Phil Taylor, never forgot (see Chapter 2). The ill-fated England Rugby World Cup squad of 2011 probably don't need to be reminded yet again of this lesson. In the words of three anonymous members of the squad,

> *'To hear one senior player in the changing room say straight after the quarter-final defeat, "There's £35,000 just gone down the toilet" made me feel sick. Money shouldn't even come into a player's mind';*

> *'You sense for some players it was more about getting caps and cash than getting better';*

> *'Too many players were chasing endorsements.'*[3]

Back in 1992, at a time when English rugby and professionalism was on the rise, the England Under-21 coach Stan Liptrot remarked, 'What's happened in England is that rugby is no longer a preparation for a piss-up.'[4] Twenty years later, maybe it was time to look again at the perils and unexpected pitfalls that professionalism has brought to the sport. With this in mind, it is interesting that one of the coaching team brought in after the debacle of the World Cup felt his first priority was to put a smile back on the players' faces. According to Andy Farrell,

> *'I am part of a coaching team that has a responsibility to bring enthusiasm and enjoyment back. The slate has been cleaned, there is no looking back and part of our role is to make sure that the culture in the first week we are together is one of drive and excitement that gets smiles back on faces.'*[5]

Team performance: Problems and solutions

'They're slow starters'

This statement may characterise teams that are not entirely sure of themselves – so they wait for the game to spark them into action, when instead they could be far more proactive than reactive. Often teams that wait for a catalyst such as a setback or a bad decision to spur them to action have developed this reactive approach because they have spent too long dwelling on how to counter the opposition instead of how to stamp their mark on the game. In these situations there may be a need to instil a greater sense of identity and hunger based on longer-term goals, and to ensure that the team shares a common sense of purpose. Practical pre-match techniques such as focusing all attention on the first five minutes ('big five') can help.

'They're poor finishers'

This can often reflect on one of two issues – either the team lacks self-belief and its capacity to win through, or the team has too much self-belief and eases up, because it thinks the contest is over. In the first case, it could be that the team is not entirely sure what it is about (e.g., does it know what its strengths or 'weapons' are?) and how to win. When the chips are down there may be a lack of confidence in the game plan or winning formula for the team as a whole and so players may start to revert to their own ways of doing things. Reinforcing team strategies and game plans can overcome this problem, and using previous occasions where the team won through will help to bolster confidence. However if the problem is more deep-seated then it may be time to reflect on more radical measures involving the make-up, and shake-up, of the team.

At the other extreme, a team that is too confident may expect that the game will eventually drift its way, rather than devising strategies to take control and move play in its direction. Again, these problems may call for radical solutions involving changes to personnel in order to alter the culture of the team, or strategies can be devised to remind the team how to take charge.

'They drift in and out of games'

As with individual players, where a team plays in fits and starts, individually and collectively, it may be useful to break the game down into much smaller units, and to make sure that evaluation looks across all aspects of the game and not just the last few minutes. Also, with 'drifting' teams, it is helpful to set an objective before the game – such as for each player to focus on the here-and-now and make a big effort to win his or her individual battle with opponents – and for the team to win each half.

'They seem to leave it all on the training pitch'

When teams seem to play better in practice than in competition, an obvious question arises. Have players developed the right preparation techniques to control their own stress levels or has this been left to chance? Are training routines artificial or have they been designed to simulate match conditions? (See also Chapter 5 for some suggestions about simulating some common distractions in practice situations.) Are players being asked to consider the big picture too much, or are they given freedom only to think of their own task – for example, the player who is their immediate opponent? There should be no reason why training performances cannot be replicated during competition and a systematic review of obstacles to this objective should be undertaken. There may be broader issues however in terms of personal motivations and time should be spent understanding these problems.

'They just haven't gelled as a unit'

If a team seems to lack any obvious sense of identity or cohesion, it may be that sufficient time has not been spent buying into a common goal, or there may be different values or agendas at work within the team. Before proceeding, it is important to make sure that task cohesion is really the issue, or do they play well together but simply choose not to mix away from their sport? Has money or other rewards got in the way? Do they know who they are? Have they forged an identity? One remedy may be to use a few key buzz words to remind the team who they are and what they are about (one example is 'BLAH' – buzzing, light, angry, honest).

'They always seem to fall at the critical hurdle'

The team that does well in early rounds of competitions but folds when it comes to the crunch game may be carrying too much baggage around with them. For example, are they burdened by the history of the club or carrying the weight of expectation because of previous failures? In these circumstances there may be a need to cocoon the team from the wider club and supporters, to define the identity from within the group of players and not by external forces or history.

Another technique is to describe a championship campaign as a series of hurdles to be overcome, each one essentially the same but with unique characteristics. A good team meets the last hurdle just like it did the first, and it has in place pre-match routines that never vary. So when the big games do come along, they are just another day – same task, just different venue and opposition. With this in mind, to avoid 'overheating' it is important not to change routines in later rounds of a competition but to consolidate them over time and as a tournament progresses.

'They're a very quiet team'

Quietness can signify two things – either a team that knows what it is about and so has no need to talk, or a team that lacks the self-belief to express itself. Which explanation is more accurate in any given case must be worked through, to find out if there is actually a problem or not. The answer lies in having a level of communication that does not ebb and flow as the tide of a game changes but is used to manage the game and the impression created. For example, if the team becomes quiet when the tide is flowing against them this is quickly picked up by the opposition as a sign of a lack of confidence.

Beforehand, it may be useful to designate key players with the responsibility to keep the 'noise level' at the right pitch across the pitch. Positions such as goalkeeper are crucial in this regard along with key players in specific areas (e.g., defence, midfield, attack). Also, bench players can be given specific responsibility for keeping the volume high. At the same time you should also consider whether there is a more deep-seated problem of management's making – they don't talk because they don't have anything to say. In other words, they are merely acting to your instructions. The remedy does not need repeating – learn to let go.

'They never seem to follow the game plan'

This is often indicative of different agendas at work within a team and often characterises either young teams (who have never been on message), or mature teams (who have drifted off message). In both situations, it is useful to identify the cliques within the team or among management. Do some players sit together, train together, or do younger and older players not mix? The solution involves gentle social engineering to mix the team up and break alliances, for example by introducing intra-team competition, re-organising changing room arrangements, travel arrangements, accommodation, etc.

'They lack flair and only do what they're told'

This may be a consequence of being too 'hands on' – whatever instructions have been given in the past have worked so why bother thinking when you just do what you are told? This can be a hard nut to crack but has to begin with an honest acceptance that a culture of dependency has been fostered and it is now starting to have an adverse effect on performance. For example, players may turn up for games expecting to be motivated by someone else. What walks into the changing room is more important than what walks out, and danger lies in placing too much emphasis on that short time in the changing room prior to games. Inspirational team talks may work occasionally and exceptionally but it is impossible for even the most eloquent coach or manager to have the same impact time after time. Instead, it is likely that a law of diminishing returns will apply – and the rest will become history!

'It's a lazy team'

Labelling any team as 'lazy' without sufficient evidence is a big mistake. However, if it becomes apparent that certain team members are not working hard enough, perhaps the label is justified. Laziness can occur in a team that has achieved too much too soon and is finding it difficult to re-energise, or a team that has set its sights too low, or a team that has become too tight or too cohesive. In each case, the solution must involve ways of shattering the collective comfort zone, piece by piece. Unexpected changes in personnel may often be called for to stem the drift towards mediocrity but often drastic action is the only real cure.

'There are one or two in the squad who just aren't team players'

In any team there will always be those who do not appear to pull in the same direction as everyone else. Dealing with these players can be very difficult and time consuming, especially when their individual talent is considerable. Eventually, there is no alternative other than to sit down with a cost/benefit balance sheet and calculate the pros and cons – i.e., what does the player *cost* in terms of collective action and what does he or she *give* in personal performance. On the basis of this analysis, hard decisions must be made but do not be fooled into assuming that yet more attention will be the solution. Further attention often simply rewards attention-seeking behaviour, and at the same time sends the wrong signal to other players. Often, the harder you try the easier it will be for the player to keep running away.

'How can I get my substitutes to make an impact?'

Increasingly, coaches and managers are becoming interested in practical ways of ensuring that their substitutes are as alert and focused as possible while they wait to be called into action in the match. This is a difficult challenge because it's hard to keep players' minds active when they're sitting on the bench. In general, however, it's helpful to ask players to look for certain patterns of play arising in their position and to encourage them to warm-up regularly by jogging along the sidelines during the game. Also, reminding a substitute about his or her strengths or 'weapons' can give them an edge when they enter the fray.

There's more!

For those who want more, here is a select list of contemporary sport psychology books that may interest you.

Andersen, M. B. (2005). *Sport Psychology in Practice*. Champaign, IL: Human Kinetics.
Brewer, B. W., & Van Raalte, J. (Eds.). (2012). *Exploring Sport and Exercise Psychology* (3rd ed.). Washington, DC: American Psychological Association.
Collins, D., Button, A., & Richards, H. (2011). *Performance Psychology: A Practitioner's Guide*. London: Churchill Livingstone Elsevier.

Cox, R. H. (2011). *Sport Psychology: Concepts and Applications*. St. Louis, MO: McGraw-Hill Publishers.

Hanrahan, S. J., & Andersen, M. B. (Eds.). (2010). *Routledge Handbook of Applied Sport Psychology*. London: Routledge.

Hemmings, B., & Holder, T. (2009). *Applied Sport Psychology: A Case-Based Approach*. Chichester, UK: John Wiley & Sons.

Horn, T. S. (2008). *Advances in Sport Psychology*. Champaign, IL: Human Kinetics.

Jowett, S., & Lavallee, D. (2006). *Social Psychology in Sport*. Champaign, IL: Human Kinetics.

Karageorghis, C., & Terry, P. (2011). *Inside Sport Psychology*. Champaign, IL: Human Kinetics.

Kremer, J., Moran, A., Walker, G., & Craig, C. (2011). *Key Concepts in Sport Psychology*. London: Sage.

Lavallee, D., Kremer, J., Moran, A., & Williams, M. (2012). *Sport Psychology: Contemporary Themes* (2nd ed.). London: Palgrave MacMillan.

Lavallee, D., Williams, J., & Jones, M. (2007). *Key Studies in Sport and Exercise Psychology*. Maidenhead, UK: Open University Press.

Mellalieu, S., & Hanton, S. (Eds.). (2009). *Advances in Applied Sport Psychology: A Review*. London: Routledge.

Moran, A. (2012). *Sport and Exercise Psychology: A Critical Introduction* (2nd ed.). London: Routledge.

Morris, T., Spittle, M., & Watt, A. P. (2005). *Imagery in Sport*. Champaign, IL: Human Kinetics.

Morris, T., & Summers, J. (2004). *Sport Psychology: Theories, Applications and Issues* (2nd ed.). Chichester, UK: John Wiley.

Morris, T., & Terry, P. (Eds.). (2011). *The New Sport and Exercise Psychology Companion*. Morgantown, WV: Fitness Information Technology.

Murphy, S. M. (2005). *The Sport Psych Handbook*. Champaign, IL: Human Kinetics.

Murphy, S. M. (Ed.). (2012). *Handbook of Sport and Performance Psychology*. Oxford, UK: Oxford University Press.

Shaw, D., Gorely, T., & Corban, R. (2005). *Sport and Exercise Psychology*. London: BIOS Academic Publishers.

Taylor, J., & Wilson, G. S. (2005). *Applying Sport Psychology*. Champaign, IL: Human Kinetics.

Tenenbaum, G., & Eklund, R. C. (2007). *Handbook of Sport Psychology* (3rd ed.). Chichester, UK: John Wiley & Sons.

Thatcher, J., Day, M., & Rahman, R. (2011). *Sport and Exercise Psychology*. Exeter, UK: Learning Matters.

Weinberg, R., & Gould, D. (2010). *Foundations of Sport and Exercise Psychology* (5th ed.). Champaign, IL: Human Kinetics.

Williams, J. M. (2010) *Applied Sport Psychology: Personal Growth to Peak Performance* (6th ed.). Maidenhead, UK: McGraw-Hill.

Notes

1 Starting out

1   http://tinyurl.com/5bn55t
2   http://tinyurl.com/cwqn2wo
3   http://tinyurl.com/d7nh7h3
4   http://tinyurl.com/c9m6oc2
5   Ibid.
6   www.bbc.co.uk/sport/0/tennis/19921333
7   A potter's tale: Any colour will do. (20 April 2002). *The Guardian*, pp. 10–11
8   http://tinyurl.com/3ck4nm5
9   http://is.gd/7EqQVf
10 Cited in MacRury, D. (1997). *Golfers on Golf.* London: Virgin Books, p. 95
11 Thelwell, R. C., & Maynard, I. W. (2003). The effects of a mental skills package on 'repeatable good performance' in cricketers. *Psychology of Sport and Exercise*, 4, 377–396.

2 The winning mind

1   Green, C. D. (2003). Psychology strikes out: Coleman R. Griffith and the Chicago Cubs. *History of Psychology*, 6, 267–283.
2   Black Knight of the fairways. (10 July 2005). *Sunday Independent*, p. 12.
3   Sheard, M. (2009). *Mental Toughness: The Mindset Behind Sporting Achievement.* London: Routledge.
4   Chen, C., & Stevenson, H. W. (1995). Motivation and mathematics achievement: A comparative study of Asian-American, Caucasian-American, and East Asian High School students. *Child Development*, 66, 1215–1234.
5   *Sunday Independent*, s8, 16 September 2007.
6   http://www.guardian.co.uk/sport/2011/sep/26/dai-greene-interview-400m-hurdles
7   McCoy, A. P. (2011). *My Autobiography by A.P. McCoy.* London: Orion.
8   http://www.telegraph.co.uk/sport/horseracing/8816953/Tony-McCoy-never-tires-of-daily-grind.html
9   http://tinyurl.com/blwq469
10 Wooden, J. (with S. Jamison) (1997). *Wooden: A Lifetime of Observations and Reflections On and Off the Court.* Lincolnwood, IL: Contemporary Books.
11 http://tinyurl.com/ccfm899
12 http://tinyurl.com/bwc6foj
13 Cited in Reinharz, P., & Anderson, B. (2000). Bring back sportsmanship. *City Journal* (Spring). Retrieved from http://is.gd/RbOmrN
14 http://www.vincelombardi.com/quotes.html
15 Harris, H. A. (1964). *Greek Athletes and Athletics.* Westport, CA: Greenwood Press.
16 http://tinyurl.com/d87oc9e

17 http://is.gd/lBfK9q
18 http://tinyurl.com/d87oc9e
19 Keane, R. (with Eamon Dunphy). (2002). *Keane: The Autobiography* (p. 181). London: Michael Joseph.
20 http://www.sikhiwiki.org/index.php/Fauja_Singh
21 See Roberts, G. C. (Ed.). (2001). *Advances in Motivation in Sport and Exercise*. Champaign, IL: Human Kinetics.
22 http://tinyurl.com/ca5ff2s
23 Ross, L. (1977). The intuitive psychologist and his shortcomings: Distortions in the attribution process. In L. Berkowitz (Ed.), *Advances in Experimental Social Psychology* (Vol. 10, pp. 174–221). New York: Academic Press.

3 Mirror gazing

1 Maslow, A. H. (1953). *Motivation and Personality*. New York: Harper & Row.
2 Porter, L. W., & Lawler, E. E. (1968). *Managerial Attitudes and Performance*. Homewood, IL: Dorsey Press.
3 Butler, R. J. (1996). *Sport Psychology in Action*. Oxford: Butterworth-Heinemann.
4 Cited in Fletcher, D. (2006). British swimming, sports psychology, and Olympic medals: It's all in the mind. *The World Swimming Coaches Association Newsletter*, 6, 5.
5 http://tinyurl.com/ch2n2dz
6 Locke, E. A. (1968). Toward a theory of task motivation and incentives. *Organizational Behaviour and Human Performance, 3*, 157–189.
7 Naber, J. (Ed.). (2005). *Awaken the Olympian Within: Stories from America's Greatest Olympic Motivators*. Irvine, CA: Griffin Publishing Group.
8 http://en.wikipedia.org/wiki/Gantt_chart

4 Hitting the zone

1 Distraught Mahan unfortunate final image of team loss for USA. (4 October 2010). Retrieved from http://tinyurl.com/cxlfze7 on 11 November 2011.
2 How relaxed Chelsea took complete control. (15 October 2005). *The Guardian* (Sport), p. 3.
3 Wheler, C. (12 May 2011). Gazza's day of madness: It's 20 years on since the moment that defined a superstar's crazy career. *Mail Online*. Retrieved from http://is.gd/hMpmnM on 11 November 2011.
4 Relaxed Woods identifies the major pressure points. (6 April 2001). *The Guardian*, p. 26.
5 Wagstaff, C., Neil, R., Mellalieu, S., & Hanton, S. (2011). Key movements in directional research in competitive anxiety. In J. Thatcher, M. Jones, & D. Lavallee (Eds.), *Coping and Emotion in Sport* (2nd ed., pp. 143–166). London: Routledge.
6 It's a kind of religion. (23 October 2004). *The Guardian*, p. 14 (Weekend Magazine).
7 Faldo dismisses fear of failure in a heartbeat. (15 July 2004). *The Daily Telegraph*, p. 3 (The Open special supplement).
8 Mitchell, K. Hard regime in gym helps Murray to find his feet on clay. (29 April 2010). *The Guardian* (Sport), p. 6.
9 O'Sullivan faces censure after walking out on Hendry match. (15 December 2006). *The Guardian* (Sport), p. 1
10 Jonny just the latest star to suffer paralysis by analysis. (11 November 2003). *The Daily Telegraph*, p. S4.
11 Seigne's only song: Je ne regrette rien. (5 October 1997). *The Sunday Times* (Sport), p. 14.
12 Kelly, L. Walton's new mountain. (26 October 1998). *Irish Independent* (Sport), p. 9
13 MacRury, D. (1997) *Golfers on Golf*. London: Virgin Books, p. 99.

14 England must find the cure for the spot-kick 'disease'. (19 May 2000). *The Guardian*, p. 35.

15 Masters, R. S., & Maxwell, J. P. (2008). The theory of reinvestment. *International Review of Sport and Exercise Psychology*, 2, 160–183.

16 McRae, D. Victoria Pendleton reveals her doubts, dreams and disappointments. (29 October 2011). *The Guardian* (Sport), p. 2. Retrieved from http://www.guardian.co.uk/sport/2011/oct/28/victoria-pendleton-interview

17 Breathe deeply and be happy with second. (27 September 1996). *The Irish Times*, p. 7.

18 Keeping cool with Michael Phelps. *BBC Sport Academy*. (2 May 2007). Retrieved from http://is.gd/rGMQMd

19 Bee, P. The golden rules. (19 August 2012). *The Sunday Times* (Style), pp. 22–23.

5 Staying focused

1 Cited in Clarke, D., & Morris, K. (2005). *Golf: The Mind Factor* (p. 63). London: Hodder & Stoughton.

2 Cited in Miller, B. (1997). *Gold Minds: The Psychology of Winning in Sport* (p. 64). Marlborough, UK: Crowood Press.

3 McIlroy's talent finds its reward in finest fashion. (21 June 2011). *The Irish Times*, pp. 20–21.

4 Alberto Contador makes decisive move and Armstrong has no reply. (19 July 2009). *The Guardian Online*. Retrieved from http://is.gd/gQTIxc on 27 November 2011.

5 Sarkar, P. Open – Federer unnerved by spectator intrusion. (7 June 2009). *ESPN Tennis*. Retrieved from http://tinyurl.com/c45g99w on 27 November 2011.

6 How to . . . psyche out a batsman. (December/January 2011). *Sky Sports Magazine*, p. 11.

7 The top 10 sporting distractions. (24 October 2004). *Sunday Times* (Sport), p. 2.

8 Oh dear, so near but so far away. (12 July 2005). *The Irish Times*, p. 21.

9 Ballengee, R. (2009). The FedExCup problem: It's not the points, it's the money. Retrieved from http://is.gd/Rp0kHJ on 24 September 2009.

10 Corry, M. Brocolli, foul focus drinks and hip-hop: How we will prepare for the big kick-off. (13 October 2007). *The Guardian* (Sport), p. 3.

11 Interview: Garry Sobers. (10 June 2002). *The Guardian* (Sport), p. 20.

12 Walsh, D. Is this the world's greatest athlete? (6 July 2008). *The Sunday Times* (Sport), pp. 12–13.

13 Fear of failure haunted me right to the last second. (1 May 2004). *The Guardian* (Sport), p. 12.

14 Kelly, L. Louis kept his head by seeing red. (21 July 2010). *Irish Independent* (Sport), p. 7.

15 Cited in Moran, A. (2009). *Learn to Win at Golf: Doing Your Best When It Matters Most*. Belfast, UK: MindCool Productions. See http://tinyurl.com/d8e5r8c

16 Holmes finds self-belief and double delight. (30 August 2004). *The Guardian*, p. 6.

17 Cited in English, A. (2006). *Munster: Our Road to Glory*. Dublin: Penguin.

18 I'm not really running, I'm not really running. (8 April 2011). *The New York Times*. Retrieved from http://tinyurl.com/avytm5 on 29 November 2011.

19 Souter, M. O'Gara gives heart to Ireland as they reach their pivotal moment. (23 March 2009). *The Times*, p. 67.

20 Cited in Clarke, D., & Morris, K. (2005). *Golf: The Mind Factor*. London: Hodder & Stoughton.

21 It's all in the hands. (20 November 2003). *The Guardian* (G2), p. 2.

22 Casey, B. Power of the mind key to curing a team with a stutter. (21 February 2011). *The Irish Times* (Sport), p. 5.

23 Whitworth, D. On the waterfront. (13 September 2008). *The Times* (Magazine), pp. 20–25.

24 Cited in Jeffries, S. A life aquatic. (24 May 2012). *The Guardian* (G2), p. 6.

6 Using your imagination

1 Walsh, D. You only get one shot at this – you can't play the game again. (29 March 2009). *Sunday Times* (Sport), p. 9.
2 Retrieved from http://is.gd/hsqUmS on 5 December 2011.
3 Fear of failure haunted me right to the last second. (1 May 2004). *The Guardian* (Sport), p. 12.
4 Moran, A., Guillot, A., MacIntyre, T., & Collet, C. (2012). Re-imagining mental imagery: Building bridges between cognitive and sport psychology. *British Journal of Psychology*, 103, 224–247. doi:10.1111/j.2044-8295.2011.02068.x
5 Phelps, M. (2008). *No Limits: The Will to Succeed*. New York: Simon & Schuster.
6 Nicklaus, J., & Boden, K. (1974). *Golf My Way*. New York: Simon & Schuster.
7 Plod and panache a recipe for success at the home of golf. (11 July 2005). *The Independent* (Sport), p. 58.
8 Murphy, S. (2005). Imagery: Inner theatre becomes reality. In S. Murphy (Ed.), *The Sport Psych Handbook* (pp. 127–151). Champaign, IL: Human Kinetics.
9 Moran, A. (2012). *Sport and Exercise Psychology: A Critical Introduction* (2nd ed.). London: Routledge.
10 Kosslyn, S., Ganis, G., & Thompson, W. L. (2001). Neural foundations of imagery. *Nature Reviews: Neuroscience*, 2, 635–642.
11 Lorey, B., Pilgramm, S., Bischoff, M., Stark, R., Vaitl, D., et al. (2011). Activation of the parieto-premotor network is associated with vivid motor imagery: A parametric fMRI study. *PLoS ONE*, 6, e20368, doI: 10.1371/journal.pone.0020368
12 Morris, T., Spittle, M., & Watt, A. (2005). *Imagery in Sport*. Champaign, IL: Human Kinetics.
13 Moran, A. P., & MacIntyre, T. (1998). There's more to an image than meets the eye: A qualitative study of kinaesthetic imagery in elite canoe-slalomists. *Irish Journal of Psychology*, 19, 406–423.
14 Pitt, N. Out of the Woods. (19 July 1998). *The Sunday Times*, p. 5.
15 Munroe-Chandler, K., & Morris, T. (2011). Imagery. In T. Morris & P. C. Terry (Eds.), *The New Sport and Exercise Psychology Companion* (pp. 275–308). Morgantown, WV: Fitness Information Technology.
16 Hall, C. (2001). Imagery in sport and exercise. In R. N. Singer, H. A. Hausenblas, & C. M. Janelle (Eds.), *Handbook of Research on Sport Psychology* (2nd ed., pp. 529–549). New York: Wiley.
17 Martin, K. A., Moritz, S. E., & Hall, C. (1999). Imagery use in sport: A literature review and applied model. *The Sport Psychologist*, 13, 245–268.
18 Van de Braam, M., & Moran, A. (in press). The prevalence and effects of negative mental imagery in tennis. *Journal of Medicine and Science in Tennis*, 16, 34–37.
19 Hemery, D. At the time, I didn't know that I'd won. (17 October 2009). *The Guardian* (Sport), p. 2.
20 Winner, D. (2012). Wayne Rooney: Beautiful game, beautiful mind. (16 May 2012). *ESPN The Magazine*. Retrieved from http://tinyurl.com/bl3uchp on 19 November 2012.
21 Ice-man Faulds keeps cool to shoot gold. (21 September 2000). *The Guardian*, p. 7.
22 Retrieved from http://www.a1sportingmemorabilia.co.uk/st-andrews-masterclass-signed-by-nick-faldo.html on 11 December 2011.
23 Carlin, J. Most Bonito. (4 June 2006). *The New York Times*. Retrieved from http://is.gd/9jmD2h on 11 December 2011.
24 Begley, S. Mind games. (24 September 2000). *Newsweek Magazine*. Retrieved from http://tinyurl.com/bwlb9hz on 11 December 2011.
25 James, W. (1890). *Principles of Psychology*. New York: Holt, Rinehart and Winston.
26 Driskell, J. E., Copper, C. M., & Moran, A. (1994). Does mental practice enhance performance? *Journal of Applied Psychology*, 79, 481–492.

27 Kremer, J., Moran, A., Walker, G., & Craig, C. (2011). *Key Concepts in Sport Psychology*. London: Sage.
28 Wakefield, C. J., Smith, D., Moran, A., & Holmes, P. (in press). Functional equivalence or behavioural matching? A critical reflection on 15 years of research using the PETTLEP model of motor imagery. *International Review of Sport and Exercise Psychology*. doi:10. 1080/1750984X.2012.724437

7 Handling setbacks and mistakes

1   Northcroft, J., & Walsh, D. England: The team that never was. (4 July 2010). *The Sunday Times* (Sport), pp. 6–7.
2   Southgate, G. We are breeding players that are looking for excuses. (4 July 2010). *The Sunday Times* (Sport), p. 7.
3   One fine day. (5 November 2006). *Sunday Tribune*, p. 31.
4   Donegan, L. The year McIlroy choked, cried and most of all grew up. (17 December 2011). *The Guardian* (Sport), p. 8.
5   Carlson, R. (1998). *The Don't Sweat the Small Stuff Workbook*. London: Hodder and Stoughton.
6   Faulty Federer beaten by masterful Murray. (14 October 2012). *ESPN UK*. Retrieved from http://tinyurl.com/bn84lg4 on 20 November 2012.
7   Cragg takes the scalp of Bekele. (31 January 2005). *The Irish Times* (Sport), p. 6.
8   Isaacson, M. Emmons loses gold on last shot again. (18 August 2008). *Los Angeles Times*. Retrieved from http://tinyurl.com/cf7gd2m on 14 December 2011.
9   Cited in 'The greatest of them all turns 65'. International Sports Press Association (AIPS) website, January 2007.
10 Cited in ibid.
11 One fine day. (5 November 2006). *Sunday Tribune*, p. 31.
12 Relax and watch the birdies. (8 June 1997). Stress Manager, supplement to *The Sunday Times*, pp. 8–9.
13 Angry Mikhail Youzhny smacks himself. (3 April 2008). *MJ Morning Show*. Retrieved from http://is.gd/Vu7khM on 14 December 2011.
14 Morgan, W. P., Ellickson, K. A., O'Connor, P. J., & Bradley, P. W. (1992). Elite male distance runners: Personality structure, mood states and performance. *Track and Field Quarterly*, 92, 59–62.
15 Lilienfeld, S. D., Lynn, S. J., Ruscio, J., & Beyerstein, B. L. (2010). *50 Great Myths of Popular Psychology*. Chichester, UK: Wiley-Blackwell.
16 Eriksson pleads with fans not to take it out on Rooney. (3 July 2006). *The Guardian* (Sport), p.1.
17 O'Sullivan to pay for obscenities. (26 April 2004). *The Daily Telegraph*, p. S12.
18 Hodge, K. (2000). *Sports Thoughts* (p. 72). Auckland, New Zealand: Reed.
19 O'Sullivan, E., & Smyth, P. J. (2002). The attacking mindset. In B. D. Hale & D. J. Collins (Eds.), *Rugby Tough* (pp. 155–170). Champaign, IL: Human Kinetics.
20 MacRury, D. (1997). *Golfers on Golf*. London: Virgin Books.
21 Gilbert, B. (with S. Jamison). (1994). *Winning Ugly: Mental Warfare in Tennis: Lessons from a Master*. New York: Fireside Books.
22 Woodward, C. (2004). *Winning! The Story of England's Rise to Rugby World Cup Glory*. London: Hodder and Stoughton.
23 Grout, J., & Perrin, S. (2004). *Mind Games*. Chichester, UK: Capstone Publishing Ltd.
24 Peterson, C., Semmel, A., von Baeyer, C., et al. (1982). The Attributional Style Questionnaire. *Cognitive Therapy and Research*, 6, 287–299.
25 Biddle, S. J., Hanrahan, S. J., & Sellars, C. (2001). Attributions: Past, present and future. In R. N. Singer, H. A. Hausenblas, & C. M. Janelle (Eds.), *Handbook of Sport Psychology* (2nd ed., pp. 444–471). New York: John Wiley.

26 Seligman, M. E. P., Nolen-Hoeksema, S., Thornton, N., & Thornton, K. M. (1990). Explanatory style as a mechanism of disappointing athletic performance. *Psychological Science*, 1, 143–146.
27 Hannigan, M. Great sporting comebacks. (23 May 2011). *The Irish Times*. Retrieved from http://tinyurl.com/bpx4zch on 15 December 2011.
28 One fine day. (5 November 2006). *Sunday Tribune*, p. 31.

8 The team

1 See http://news.bbc.co.uk/sport1/hi/other_sports/sailing/4246831.stm
2 Forsyth, D. (2010). *Group Dynamics* (5th ed.). Belmont, CA: Wadsworth.
3 See http://content-uk.cricinfo.com/ci/content/player/9187.html
4 Welcome to Leicester where a punch from the captain is just a sign that you've arrived. (19 May 2007). *The Guardian*, p. 35. Retrieved from http://is.gd/RtqbrZ
5 Ibid.
6 Tuckman, B. (1965). Development sequence in small groups. *Psychological Bulletin*, 63, 384–399.
7 Baron, R. S. (2005). So right it's wrong: Groupthink and the ubiquitous nature of polarized group decision making. In M. P. Zanna (Ed.), *Advances in Experimental Social Psychology* (Vol. 37, pp. 219–253). San Diego, CA. Elsevier Academic Press.
8 http://is.gd/W1PVnA
9 Clough, B. (with J. Sadler). (2002). *Cloughie: Walking on Water*. London: Headline.
10 http://en.wikipedia.org/wiki/Kamp_Staaldraad
11 Courneya, K. S., & Carron, A. V. (1992). Home advantage in sport competitions: A literature review. *Journal of Sport and Exercise Psychology*, 14, 13–27.
12 Jones, M. V., et al. (2007). All the world's a stage: Impact of an audience on sport performers. In S. Jowett & D. Lavallee (Eds.), *Social Psychology in Sport* (pp. 91–102). Champaign, IL: Human Kinetics.
13 Triplett, N. (1898). The dynamogenic factors in pacemaking and competition. *American Journal of Psychology*, 9, 505–523.
14 Lavallee, D., Moran, A., Kremer, J., & Williams, A. M. (2012). *Sport Psychology Contemporary Themes* (2nd ed.). London: Palgrave MacMillian.
15 Michaels, J. W., Blommel, J. M., Brocato, R. M., Linkous, R. A., & Rowe, J. S. (1982). Social facilitation and inhibition in a natural setting. *Replications in Social Psychology*, 2, 21–24.
16 Lavallee, D., Moran, A., Kremer, J., & Williams, A. M. (2012). *Sport Psychology Contemporary Themes* (2nd ed.). London: Palgrave MacMillian.
17 Cited in Hodge, K. (2000). *Sports Thoughts*. Auckland, New Zealand: Reed.
18 Clough, B. (with J. Sadler). (2002). *Cloughie: Walking on Water*. London: Headline.

9 Leading and managing

1 www.nelsonmandelas.com/mandela-quotes.php
2 http://www.rateitall.com/i-53312-john-wooden.aspx
3 Wooden, J. (with S. Jamison) (1997). *Wooden: A Lifetime of Observations and Reflections On and Off the Court*. Lincolnwood, IL: Contemporary Books.
4 Wooden, J. (with S. Jamison) (2007). *The Essential Wooden: A Lifetime of Lessons on Leaders and Leadership*. New York: McGraw-Hill.
5 Woodward, C. (2004). *Winning!* London: Hodder and Stoughton.
6 Marcotti, G. (2001). Made not born. *The Sunday Tribune* (Sport), 7 October, p. 9.
7 Ibid.
8 Clough, B. (with J. Sadler). (2002). *Cloughie: Walking on Water*. London: Headline.
9 Ibid.

10 Duffy, P. J., Lyons, D. C., Moran, A. P., Warrington, G. D., & MacManus, C. (2006). How we got here: Perceived influences on the development and success of international athletes. *Irish Journal of Psychology,* 27 (3–4), 150–167.
11 Maraniss, D. (1999). *When Pride Still Mattered: A Life of Vince Lombardi.* New York: Touchstone.
12 Retrieved from main.wgbh.org/imax/shackleton/sirernest.html
13 Chelladurai, P. (1993). Leadership. In R. N. Singer, M. Murphey, & L. K. Tennant (Eds.), *Handbook of Research in Sport Psychology* (pp. 647–671). New York: Macmillan.
14 Talking the talk. (15 April 2007). *The Observer* (Sport), p. 12.
15 http://tinyurl.com/bwhuzlm
16 Mottram, D. (2010). *Drugs in Sport* (5th ed.). London: Routledge.
17 http://tinyurl.com/c9547oq

10 The end?

1 McCoy, A. P. (2002). *McCoy: The Autobiography* (pp. 265–266). London: Michael Joseph.
2 http://tinyurl.com/6uyte7b
3 McCoy, A. P. (2002). *McCoy: The Autobiography* (p. 266). London: Michael Joseph.
4 Robert Louis Stevenson (1881). Quotation from *Virginibus Puerisque.*
5 Kipling, R. (1895). *If.* (First published in the *Brother Square Toes* chapter of *Rewards and Fairies,* 1910).
6 http://www.guardian.co.uk/sport/2011/nov/20/mark-cavendish-london-olympics-2012
7 Wooden, J. (with S. Jamison) (2007). *The Essential Wooden: A Lifetime of Lessons on Leaders and Leadership.* New York: McGraw-Hill.
8 Psychologist Mourinho inspires with group therapy. (1 April 2007). *The Sunday Times,* p. 2 (Sport).

Problems and solutions

1 Casey in prime condition for best shot at green jacket. (4 April 2007). *The Guardian,* p. 32.
2 Carron, A. V., Prapavessis, H., & Grove, J. R. (1994). Group effects and self-handicapping. *Journal of Sport and Exercise Psychology,* 16, 246–257.
3 http://tinyurl.com/cvnb4zk
4 http://is.gd/EWSHey
5 http://is.gd/6KqOBe

Index